Getting Started with MariaDB
Second Edition

Explore the powerful features of MariaDB with practical examples

Daniel Bartholomew

[PACKT] open source✲
PUBLISHING   community experience distilled

BIRMINGHAM - MUMBAI

Getting Started with MariaDB
Second Edition

First published: June 2015

Production reference: 1120615

Published by Packt Publishing Ltd.
Livery Place
35 Livery Street
Birmingham B3 2PB, UK.

ISBN 978-1-78528-412-0

www.packtpub.com

Credits

Author

Daniel Bartholomew

Reviewers

David Chanial

Emilien Kenler

Giacomo Picchiarelli

Commissioning Editor

Kartikey Pandey

Acquisition Editor

Usha Iyer

Content Development Editor

Siddhesh Salvi

Technical Editor

Shashank Desai

Copy Editors

Sarang Chari

Sonia Mathur

Project Coordinator

Nidhi Joshi

Proofreader

Safis Editing

Indexer

Monica Ajmera Mehta

Production Coordinator

Arvindkumar Gupta

Cover Work

Arvindkumar Gupta

About the Author

Daniel Bartholomew has been using Linux since 1997 and databases since 1998. In addition to this book, he has also written *MariaDB Cookbook*, *Packt Publishing*, and dozens of articles for various magazines, including *The Linux Journal*, *Linux Pro*, *Ubuntu User*, and *Tux*. He became involved with the MariaDB project shortly after it began in early 2009 and continues to be involved to this day. He currently works for MariaDB, Inc. and splits his time between managing MariaDB releases, documentation, and maintaining various bits and pieces that keep the MariaDB project running smoothly.

About the Reviewers

David Chanial is a French autodidactic system administrator and programmer. He has been setting up high-availability hosting solutions for years, especially using Gentoo Linux, Apache/Nginx, PHP, MariaDB/MySQL, and Python/Perl/C.

Having sold the French company Euro Web (hosting, dedicated servers, managed services, and consulting) in 2011, which he cofounded and managed on a technical level from 2003, he spent some time working as a consultant and a system/API developer through his company, DaviXX.

Since 2013–2014, in addition to working independently through his company on projects using Ansible, MariaDB, Django, and embedded electronics and reviewing books such as *MariaDB High Performance*, *Packt Publishing*, David held the position of a system administrator and network director at Believe Digital Group, managing database issues (big data), network infrastructure, and homemade storage solutions.

Emilien Kenler, after working on small web projects, began focusing on game development in 2008 while he was in high school. Until 2011, he worked for different groups and specialized in system administration.

In 2011, while studying computer science engineering, he founded a company that sold Minecraft servers. He created a lightweight IaaS (`https://github.com/HostYourCreeper/`) based on new technologies, such as Node.js and RabbitMQ.

Thereafter, he worked at TaDaweb as a system administrator, building its infrastructure and creating tools to manage deployments and monitoring.

In 2014, he began a new adventure at Wizcorp, Tokyo. In 2014, Emilien graduated from the University of Technology of Compiègne, France.

Emilien has also contributed as a reviewer on *Learning Nagios 4*, *MariaDB High Performance*, *OpenVZ Essentials*, and *Vagrant Virtual Development Environment Cookbook*, all books by Packt Publishing.

Giacomo Picchiarelli is a test and software engineer with 6 years of experience in designing data-driven applications and MySQL administration. He has a strong background in Linux systems and test-driven development.

www.PacktPub.com

Support files, eBooks, discount offers, and more

For support files and downloads related to your book, please visit www.PacktPub.com.

Did you know that Packt offers eBook versions of every book published, with PDF and ePub files available? You can upgrade to the eBook version at www.PacktPub.com and as a print book customer, you are entitled to a discount on the eBook copy. Get in touch with us at service@packtpub.com for more details.

At www.PacktPub.com, you can also read a collection of free technical articles, sign up for a range of free newsletters and receive exclusive discounts and offers on Packt books and eBooks.

https://www2.packtpub.com/books/subscription/packtlib

Do you need instant solutions to your IT questions? PacktLib is Packt's online digital book library. Here, you can search, access, and read Packt's entire library of books.

Why subscribe?

- Fully searchable across every book published by Packt
- Copy and paste, print, and bookmark content
- On demand and accessible via a web browser

Free access for Packt account holders

If you have an account with Packt at www.PacktPub.com, you can use this to access PacktLib today and view 9 entirely free books. Simply use your login credentials for immediate access.

Table of Contents

Preface

Databases are all around us. Almost every website we visit and nearly every store we shop at has a database (or several) working quietly behind the scenes. The same goes for banks, hospitals, government agencies, theaters, doctors, hospitals, amusement parks, and police departments. All use databases to store, sort, and analyze their own particular information.

This information comes in many forms and can be anything that can be stored electronically inside a computer. This includes books, catalogs, addresses, names, dates, finances, pictures, money, passwords, documents, preferences, tweets, posts, likes, blogs, articles, and much more. Databases are one of the foundational pillars of the modern electronic world.

Your posts on Facebook and tweets on Twitter are stored in a database. All your financial information in your bank is stored in a database. Your purchase history at your favorite online retailer is too. How about your progress in your favorite online game? You guessed it. What about the record of when you last paid your water bill? That too! You just can't get away from databases. They are, quite literally, everywhere.

There is a new database that has caught the attention of the database community over the past few years like few others have. First released in 2009, its name is MariaDB— named after the youngest daughter of its creator, Michael "Monty" Widenius.

MariaDB may be younger than the databases it is often compared with, but it has a stellar parentage. It's a next-generation evolution of the popular MySQL database, also created by Monty (you may have heard of it, but don't worry if you haven't).

MariaDB is open source. This means that the source code is freely downloadable and is governed by a license that helps ensure the source code stays free and open to all. The MariaDB developers have also kindly provided installers for various operating systems.

Since its first release, MariaDB has gained a large, loyal following faster than almost any other database. Today, it powers tens of thousands of websites, big and small, and is the database of choice for many companies in a wide variety of industries around the world with hundreds of thousands of users.

The great news is that we can install and use it ourselves, right now, on our personal laptop and desktop computers. For all of its power—and MariaDB is a very powerful and capable database, make no mistake—it is very easy to install and use.

This book provides an introduction to MariaDB that is enough to get us started. Don't worry if you've never used a database before - this book covers everything you need to know, and before you know it, you'll be on your way to becoming an expert database administrator (DBA). But even if you never move beyond just tinkering or playing around with MariaDB, you'll learn about one of the fundamental technologies of our times.

Not a bad accomplishment over a weekend or two.

What this book covers

Chapter 1, Installing MariaDB, explains how to install MariaDB on Windows, Linux, and Mac OS X.

Chapter 2, Configuring MariaDB, explains the basics of configuring MariaDB, including the location of the configuration files and how to set common configuration options.

Chapter 3, Securing MariaDB, provides an overview of the best practices for MariaDB security, including how to easily secure a new MariaDB installation.

Chapter 4, Administering MariaDB, explains how to add and administer MariaDB user accounts.

Chapter 5, Using MariaDB – Databases and Tables, covers the commands used to create, update, and delete databases and tables.

Chapter 6, Using MariaDB – Inserting, Updating, and Deleting, covers the commands used to add, update, and delete data from our database tables.

Chapter 7, Using MariaDB – Retrieving Data, covers the commands used to retrieve data from our database tables, including filtering, searching, sorting, joining, and summarizing the data.

Chapter 8, *Maintaining MariaDB*, explains how to maintain your MariaDB database and keep it running smoothly.

Appendix, *MariaDB Next Steps*, provides you with a list of various online resources available to help you on your way to becoming a MariaDB expert.

What you need for this book

To get the most out of this book, you will need a computer with Windows, any version from XP to Windows 8 would do; Mac OS X; or one of the Linux distributions: Ubuntu, Debian, Fedora, CentOS, or Red Hat. MariaDB runs on many more operating systems and distributions, but these are the ones that are specifically mentioned and discussed in this book.

To install MariaDB, you will need an Internet connection and the necessary administrative rights to install software.

To edit MariaDB configuration files, you will need a text editor. Notepad is a good universal choice on Windows. TextEdit and TextWrangler work well on Mac OS X. There are many excellent text editors on Linux, just pick a favorite: Vim, gedit, nano, pluma, and emacs are all good choices. A word processor, such as Word, Wordpad, OpenOffice, Pages, or LibreOffice, will not work.

No other software is required.

Who this book is for

This book is for anyone who wants to learn more about databases in general, and/or MariaDB in particular. To get the most out of this book, you only need to be comfortable installing software on your computer, editing files with a text editor, and using the command line and terminal. Prior database experience is not required.

Conventions

In this book, you will find a number of text styles that distinguish between different kinds of information. Here are some examples of these styles and an explanation of their meaning.

Code words in text, database table names, folder names, filenames, file extensions, pathnames, dummy URLs, user input, and Twitter handles are shown as follows: "As mentioned previously, the ZIP files are similar to the Linux binary `.tar.gz` files and they are only recommended for those who know that they want it."

A block of code is set as follows:

```
CREATE TABLE employees (
    id INT NOT NULL AUTO_INCREMENT PRIMARY KEY,
    surname VARCHAR(100),
    givenname VARCHAR(100),
    pref_name VARCHAR(50),
    birthday DATE COMMENT 'approximate birthday OK'
);
```

Any command-line input or output is written as follows:

```
brew doctor
```

New terms and **important words** are shown in bold. Words that you see on the screen, for example, in menus or dialog boxes, appear in the text like this: "The **Install as service** box is checked by default, and it is recommended to keep it that way so that MariaDB starts up when the computer is booted."

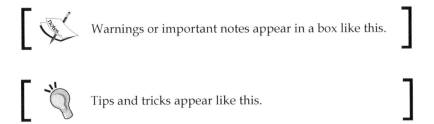

> Warnings or important notes appear in a box like this.

> Tips and tricks appear like this.

Reader feedback

Feedback from our readers is always welcome. Let us know what you think about this book—what you liked or disliked. Reader feedback is important for us as it helps us develop titles that you will really get the most out of.

To send us general feedback, simply e-mail feedback@packtpub.com, and mention the book's title in the subject of your message.

If there is a topic that you have expertise in and you are interested in either writing or contributing to a book, see our author guide at www.packtpub.com/authors.

Customer support

Now that you are the proud owner of a Packt book, we have a number of things to help you to get the most from your purchase.

Downloading the example code

You can download the example code files from your account at `http://www.packtpub.com` for all the Packt Publishing books you have purchased. If you purchased this book elsewhere, you can visit `http://www.packtpub.com/support` and register to have the files e-mailed directly to you.

Errata

Although we have taken every care to ensure the accuracy of our content, mistakes do happen. If you find a mistake in one of our books—maybe a mistake in the text or the code—we would be grateful if you could report this to us. By doing so, you can save other readers from frustration and help us improve subsequent versions of this book. If you find any errata, please report them by visiting `http://www.packtpub.com/submit-errata`, selecting your book, clicking on the **Errata Submission Form** link, and entering the details of your errata. Once your errata are verified, your submission will be accepted and the errata will be uploaded to our website or added to any list of existing errata under the Errata section of that title.

To view the previously submitted errata, go to `https://www.packtpub.com/books/content/support` and enter the name of the book in the search field. The required information will appear under the **Errata** section.

Piracy

Piracy of copyrighted material on the Internet is an ongoing problem across all media. At Packt, we take the protection of our copyright and licenses very seriously. If you come across any illegal copies of our works in any form on the Internet, please provide us with the location address or website name immediately so that we can pursue a remedy.

Please contact us at `copyright@packtpub.com` with a link to the suspected pirated material.

We appreciate your help in protecting our authors and our ability to bring you valuable content.

Questions

If you have a problem with any aspect of this book, you can contact us at `questions@packtpub.com`, and we will do our best to address the problem.

1
Installing MariaDB

Before we can start using MariaDB, we have to install it. The MariaDB source code can be compiled to run on a wide variety of different platforms and system architectures, but there are pre-compiled packages available for Windows and Linux, which make the process easier.

In addition to the source code, there are several other package types, such as:

- Windows MSI packages
- Linux YUM packages
- Linux APT packages
- Linux and Windows binaries

The Windows MSI packages are for computers and servers running from Windows XP to Windows 8. The Linux `.rpm` packages are used with distributions such as Fedora, CentOS, and Red Hat that use the **Yellow Dog Updater modified** (**YUM**) package manager. Linux `.deb` packages are used with distributions such as Debian and Ubuntu, which use the **Advanced Packaging Tool** (**APT**) package manager. We will cover how to install all these types in this chapter.

We will cover the fourth type, the Linux and Windows binaries, only briefly. These packages are mainly useful to experienced users of MariaDB who have non-standard custom setups on their database servers. The Windows binaries come in a ZIP file (`.zip`) and the Linux binaries in a gzipped tar file (`.tar.gz`), sometimes called a binary tarball.

Even though the MariaDB binaries are recommended for more experienced users, installing them is not especially difficult. Check the following links for the official instructions to install the Linux and Windows binary packages, respectively:

- `https://mariadb.com/kb/en/installing-mariadb-binary-tarballs`
- `https://mariadb.com/kb/en/installing-mariadb-windows-zip-packages`

We will also cover how to install MariaDB on Mac OS X. Packages for this operating system supplied by a third party, not by the MariaDB developers.

The choice of which MariaDB package to install is an easy one—just use whichever one is appropriate for your system. If you are using Windows, use the MSI package, for Ubuntu or Debian, use the APT packages, and for Red Hat, Fedora, or CentOS, use the YUM packages.

The rest of this chapter contains instructions for each type but before we get to that, we need to talk about series. And no, it has nothing to do with baseball, but it does lend itself to a baseball analogy.

So in short, the topics of the remaining sections in this chapter are as follows:

- Choosing a MariaDB series
- Installing MariaDB on Windows
- Installing MariaDB on Mac OS X
- Installing MariaDB on Debian, Ubuntu, and Linux Mint
- Installing MariaDB on Fedora, Red Hat, and CentOS
- Installing MariaDB on other Linux distributions
- MariaDB package security
- After the installation
- Troubleshooting installation issues

Feel free to jump around and only read the sections that directly pertain to you and your chosen operating system.

Choosing a MariaDB series

The development of MariaDB proceeds along multiple development tracks, called **series**. There is a stable series and several maintenance series. Often, there is also a development series. This is similar to the Debian GNU/Linux practice of having stable, testing, and unstable versions.

The development series

The development series of MariaDB is where the major new features and capabilities are introduced. Think of this like minor league baseball where the upcoming future stars are introduced and are improved and honed to perfection. At any given time, the quality of the current development release could range from *Alpha* (which has no guarantees that it will even work reliably) to *Beta* (which is feature-complete but generally needs a lot of bug fixing and testing) to *Release Candidate* (which is ready for general use except for some additional testing and minor bug fixing).

During the development cycle, there will generally be several Alpha releases, where new features are introduced, followed by a couple of Beta releases where the code is refined and polished, followed by one or two Release Candidate releases where the final fixes and polishing take place. The final step for any development series is when it is declared stable and moves into the major league stable series.

> If the current development series release of MariaDB is a Release Candidate, we may want to choose that over the current stable release. Otherwise, it is generally best to stick with whatever the current stable release is.

The stable series

For most users just starting out, whatever series is marked stable is the one to use. This is the major league series, the best and most complete version currently available. After a development series has reached a sufficient level of quality to be considered stable, it is promoted to this series and becomes the recommended version of MariaDB.

After being marked as stable, the MariaDB Foundation has a policy that the series will be well supported with bug and security fixes for a period of at least 5 years. This is regardless of whether it is the current stable series or if it is one of the maintenance series. It all depends on when it first becomes stable.

The maintenance series

When a series moves from development to stable, the series that was the current stable one is moved to become a maintenance series. This means that it will still receive bug fixes for the rest of its 5-year maintenance period but it is no longer the recommended or preferred release of MariaDB. Think of it as the hall of fame—full of great previous releases of MariaDB, which while still excellent, have been replaced by a new generation. At any given time, there may be three, four, or more MariaDB major versions in the maintenance series.

Most Linux distributions include MariaDB in their package repositories, either as the default MySQL-compatible database, or as an alternative choice. The version of MariaDB that they include is up to them, and while it is sometimes the most recent stable version of MariaDB, it is often one of the more recent major versions in the maintenance series.

We'll now go through the installation of MariaDB for each of the major operating systems. First Windows, then Mac OS X, then Debian GNU/Linux and Ubuntu Linux, followed by Fedora, Red Hat, and CentOS Linux, and lastly, other Linux distributions.

Installing MariaDB on Windows

There are two types of MariaDB downloads for Windows: ZIP files and MSI packages. As mentioned previously, the ZIP files are similar to the Linux binary `.tar.gz` files and they are only recommended for those who know that they want it.

If we are starting out with MariaDB for Windows, it is recommended to use the MSI packages. The following are the steps to do just that:

1. Download the MSI package from `https://downloads.mariadb.org/` location. First click on the series that we want (whatever is the current stable version, most likely), then locate the Windows 64-bit or Windows 32-bit MSI package. For most Windows PCs, the 64-bit MSI package is probably the one that we want, especially if we have more than 4 GB of RAM. If you're unsure, the 32-bit package will work on both 32-bit and 64-bit Windows computers.

2. Once the download has finished, launch the MSI installer by double-clicking on it. Depending on the local Windows settings, you may be promoted to launch the installer automatically. The installer will walk us through installing MariaDB.

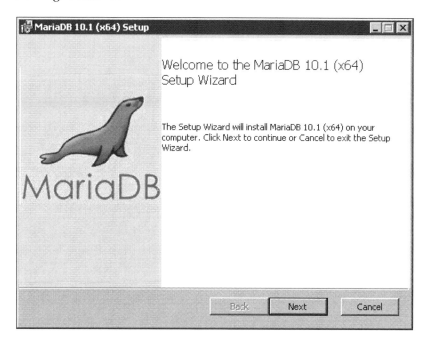

3. If we are installing MariaDB for the first time, we must be sure to set the MariaDB root user password when prompted. This is done by checking the **Modify password for database user 'root'** checkbox and then filling in our chosen password two times in the provided textboxes.

4. Unless you need to, don't check the **Enable access from remote machines for 'root' user** or the **Create An Anonymous Account** checkboxes. We'll cover creating regular user accounts in *Chapter 4, Administering MariaDB*.

5. The **Use UTF8 as the default server's character set** checkbox is unchecked by default, but it's a good idea to check it, as shown in the following screenshot:

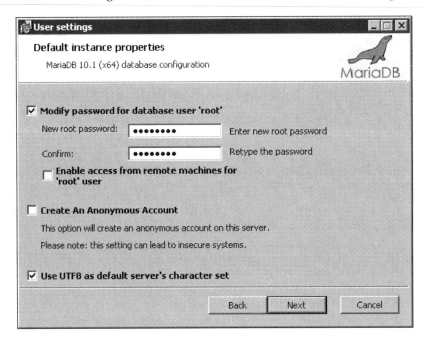

6. The **Install as service** box is checked by default, and it is recommended to keep it that way so that MariaDB starts up when the computer is booted.

7. The **Service Name** textbox has the default value MySQL for compatibility reasons, but we can rename it if we like. This name is what Windows uses to identify the running service, and it does not affect MariaDB so, it is okay to rename or keep it as the default name.

8. Check the **Enable networking** option if you need to access your databases from a different computer. If you don't need remote access, it's best to uncheck this box. As with the service name, there is a default TCP port, number 3306, which we can change if we want to, but it is usually best to stick with the default unless there is a specific reason not to.

9. The **Optimize for transactions** checkbox is also checked by default. This is the recommended setting, as shown here:

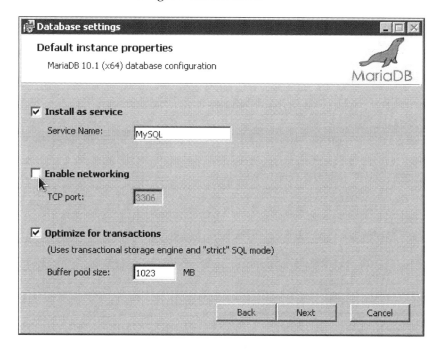

10. One easy way to help the MariaDB developers is to check the **Enable the Feedback plugin** checkbox, as shown in the following screenshot. When enabled, the feedback plugin submits anonymous usage information to the MariaDB Foundation. This information includes things such as what plugins are enabled, how much memory MariaDB uses, and the operating system that we are using. MariaDB developers use this information to guide MariaDB development.

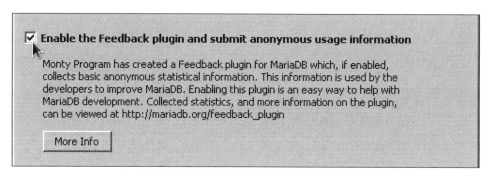

11. There are other settings that we can make through the installer. All of them can be changed later by editing the `my.ini` file. We will be covering this in *Chapter 2, Configuring MariaDB*, so we don't need to worry about them right away.

12. If our version of Windows has user account control enabled, a pop-up window will appear during the installation asking if we want to allow the installer to install MariaDB. For obvious reasons, we will need to click on **Yes**.

13. Once the installation is complete, there will be a `MariaDB` folder added to the start or the programs menu. There will be various links under this, including one to the `mysql` command-line client application. We will be using this application in *Chapters 5-7*.

> If we already have an older version of MariaDB or MySQL running on our machine, we will be prompted to upgrade the data files to the correct format for the version we are installing. It is highly recommended to do that.

14. Eventually, we will be presented with a dialog box containing an installation complete message and a **Finish** button. At this point, MariaDB is installed and running on our Windows-based computer. Congratulations! Click on **Finish** to quit the installer.

To install MariaDB on Mac OS X or Linux, read on; otherwise, feel free to skip those sections.

Installing MariaDB on Mac OS X

One of the easiest ways to install MariaDB on Mac OS X is to use Homebrew, which is an open source package manager for that platform. Before you can install it, however, you need to prepare your system. The first thing you need to do is install Xcode—Apple's integrated development environment. It's available for free from the Mac App Store.

Once Xcode is installed, you can install brew. Full instructions are available on the Homebrew Project website at `http://brew.sh` but the basic procedure is to open a terminal and run the following command:

```
ruby -e "$(curl -fsSL
https://raw.githubusercontent.com/Homebrew/install/master/install)"
```

The preceding command downloads the installer and runs it. Once the initial installation is complete, we run the following command to make sure everything is set up properly:

```
brew doctor
```

The output of the preceding command will tell us about any potential issues, along with suggestions to fix them. Once brew is working properly, we can install MariaDB with the following commands:

```
brew update
brew install mariadb
```

 There is no option to choose a specific MariaDB series; whatever is the current version in brew is the one that will be installed. Also, brew will not prompt you to set a database user password during installation, this is dangerous, so be sure to set one immediately afterwards, following the instructions in *Chapter 3, Securing MariaDB*.

MariaDB will not automatically be started after installation. To do so, we run the following commands:

```
ln -sfv /usr/local/opt/mariadb/*.plist ~/Library/LaunchAgents
launchctl load ~/Library/LaunchAgents/homebrew.mxcl.mariadb.plist
```

To stop MariaDB, we use the unload command, as follows:

```
launchctl unload ~/Library/LaunchAgents/homebrew.mxcl.mariadb.plist
```

To learn about installing MariaDB on Linux, read on. Otherwise, skip to the *After the installation* section at the end of this chapter.

Installing MariaDB on Debian, Ubuntu, and Linux Mint

The procedure to install MariaDB on Debian GNU/Linux, Ubuntu, and Linux Mint is easy and starts with a visit to the repository configuration tool from:

```
https://downloads.mariadb.org/mariadb/repositories
```

This tool is used for APT-based Linux distributions, such as Debian, Ubuntu, and Mint; Yum-based Linux distributions, such as Fedora, CentOS, and Red Hat; and other distributions that have support for MariaDB built-in, such as Mageia, Arch Linux, Suse, openSUSE, and others.

Many Linux distributions offer MariaDB in their repositories either as the default MySQL-compatible database or as an alternative choice. The instructions here will install MariaDB directly from the MariaDB repositories instead of from your Linux distribution's repositories.

Before using the tool, we need to know which version of Ubuntu, Debian, or Mint we are currently using. If you do not know, an easy way to find out is with the following command:

```
cat /etc/lsb-release
```

The output will be similar to the following:

```
DISTRIB_ID=Ubuntu

DISTRIB_RELEASE=14.04

DISTRIB_CODENAME=trusty

DISTRIB_DESCRIPTION="Ubuntu 14.04.1 LTS"
```

This example output shows that the computer is running Ubuntu 14.04.1 LTS "Trusty". So, using the repository configuration tool, we will click on **Ubuntu**, then **14.04 LTS "trusty"**, and then on the MariaDB series we want to install. Lastly, we will click on the mirror we want to use. The tool will then output three pieces of text. The first contains the commands to add the MariaDB repository to our system. The second contains the commands to actually install MariaDB. The third block of text contains alternative instructions in case adding the repository using the first set did not work.

For example, the generated commands for adding a repository for MariaDB 10.1 for Ubuntu 14.04 LTS "trusty" and using the osuosl mirror are as follows:

```
sudo apt-get install software-properties-common
sudo apt-key adv --recv-keys \
--keyserver hkp://keyserver.ubuntu.com:80 0xcbcb082a1bb943db
sudo add-apt-repository \
'deb http://ftp.osuosl.org/pub/mariadb/repo/10.0/ubuntu trusty main'
```

The first command installs the software-properties-common package if it is not already installed. This package contains the add-apt-repository command we use to install the repository. The second command imports the GPG encryption key that is used to sign MariaDB packages. For more information about this key, see the *MariaDB package security* section later in this chapter. The third command adds the repository.

Now that the repository is configured, we can install MariaDB using the following installation commands:

```
sudo apt-get update
sudo apt-get install mariadb-server
```

The `mariadb-server` package depends on the other MariaDB packages, so these two commands are all we need to install MariaDB. Once the second `apt-get` command finishes, MariaDB will be installed and running.

To learn about installing MariaDB on Fedora, Red Hat, and CentOS, read on. Otherwise, jump ahead to the *MariaDB package security* section if you're interested in the MariaDB GPG signing keys, or skip to the *After the installation* section if you want to start using MariaDB right away.

Installing MariaDB on Fedora, Red Hat, and CentOS

The procedure to install MariaDB on Fedora, Red Hat, and CentOS makes use of the **Yellowdog Updater, Modified (YUM)** package manager. There are two steps: first, create a repo file for MariaDB and second, install MariaDB.

To generate the required text for the repo file, we will visit the MariaDB repository configuration tool from:

```
https://downloads.mariadb.org/mariadb/repositories/
```

 This tool is used for APT-based Linux distributions, such as Debian, Ubuntu, and Mint; Yum-based Linux distributions, such as Fedora, CentOS, and Red Hat; and other distributions that have support for MariaDB built-in, such as Mageia, Arch Linux, Suse, openSUSE, and others.

To generate the text, we simply click on the distribution we are using, the distribution release we are using, and the version of MariaDB we want to install. After doing so, the contents of the appropriate repo file will be displayed.

For example, the text generated for MariaDB 10.1 on the 64-bit version of CentOS 7 is as follows:

```
# MariaDB 10.1 CentOS repository list
# http://mariadb.org/mariadb/repositories/
[mariadb]
name = MariaDB
baseurl = http://yum.mariadb.org/10.1/centos7-amd64
gpgkey=https://yum.mariadb.org/RPM-GPG-KEY-MariaDB
gpgcheck=1
```

The gpgkey line tells YUM where the GPG signing key is located. The gpgcheck=1 line directs YUM to always use the signing key to verify the MariaDB packages.

The first time we install MariaDB, our system will not have the key, so YUM will have to download and install it. Since YUM has never used the key before, it will ask for confirmation whether it is OK to import the key. See the *MariaDB package security* section for more information on the MariaDB GPG signing key.

We copy and paste the generated text into a file using our favorite text editor. Naming the file descriptively, such as MariaDB.repo, is recommended. Once the file is created, we then move it to the /etc/yum.repos.d/ folder using a command similar to the following one:

```
sudo mv -vi MariaDB.repo /etc/yum.repos.d/
```

Once the file is in place, we are ready to install MariaDB. This is as simple as the following:

```
sudo yum install MariaDB-server MariaDB-client
```

The capitalization of the package names is important because if we type mariadb-server instead of MariaDB-server, we will either get a package cannot be found error or, if we are using a distribution that includes MariaDB, we will get the distribution version of MariaDB instead of the version from the MariaDB project.

YUM will gather in all of the dependencies for MariaDB and present us with a list of everything that needs to be installed to install MariaDB. The following screenshot shows this:

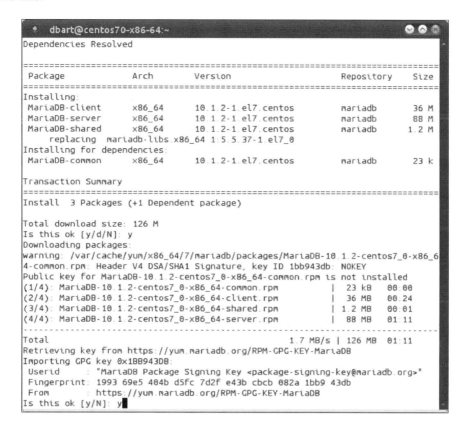

After answering y, the installation will get going and we will be prompted to accept the GPG signing key. We will verify the fingerprint with y. YUM will then continue downloading and installing MariaDB and will end with a Complete! message.

As a final step of the installation, we start MariaDB with the following command:

```
sudo /etc/init.d/mysql start
```

If everything has gone well, we will see output similar to the following:

```
[dbart@centos70-x86-64 ~]$ sudo /etc/init.d/mysql start
```

```
Starting MySQL.. SUCCESS!
```

MariaDB is now installed and running.

Jump ahead to the *MariaDB package security* section if you're interested in the MariaDB GPG signing key, or skip to the *After the installation* section if you want to start using MariaDB right away.

Installing MariaDB on other Linux distributions

MariaDB is available on more Linux distributions than just the ones listed previously in this chapter, and even if no formal packages are provided, the MariaDB developers provide generic Linux binaries that work with many versions of Linux. Instructions on how to install and use the generic binaries are available from:

```
https://mariadb.com/kb/en/mariadb/installing-mariadb-binary-tarballs/
```

Before installing these generic packages, however, it is worth your while to look in your distribution's package manager to see if MariaDB is already there.

MariaDB package security

The packages provided by the MariaDB developers are signed with a security key so that they can be verified by package managers such as yum and apt. The key signing and verification infrastructure on Linux is called **Gnu Privacy Guard** (**GPG**). It is a compatible open source version of **Pretty Good Privacy** (**PGP**), which is an industry standard data encryption, decryption, and verification system.

The identification number (GPG ID) of the MariaDB signing key is `0xcbcb082a1bb943db`. For longtime users of GPG, this ID may seem a little long. That's because, until recently, it was common to share a short form of the GPG ID. This is discouraged now because of a GPG vulnerability discovered a couple years ago; however, many utilities will still display the short form by default. The long form of the ID is more secure, so this is what the MariaDB developers share when talking about the key. But, in case we want it, the short form of the ID is `1BB943DB` (it's just the last eight characters of the long form ID). For the extra cautious, the full key fingerprint is:

```
1993 69E5 404B D5FC 7D2F E43B CBCB 082A 1BB9 43DB
```

The key IDs and fingerprint are also posted in the MariaDB Knowledge Base, which is the official location of the MariaDB documentation and is available from:

```
https://mariadb.com/kb/en/mariadb/gpg/
```

By checking the signature of the packages, Linux package managers, and more importantly, WE can verify whether the package that comes from the MariaDB developers and hasn't been tampered with since they created it.

When configuring the MariaDB repository on Debian and Ubuntu and during the initial MariaDB install on Fedora, Red Hat, and CentOS, an important task is to import the signing key. It's a good idea to verify the key by comparing it to the IDs and the fingerprint when doing so. Thankfully, this is a one-time operation. Once the key is imported, the process is fully automatic. We will only be notified if the signature check fails.

For MariaDB Windows, binary Linux, and the MariaDB source code files, we can verify them in two ways, first is by comparing the `md5sum` of the file we downloaded with the `md5sum` posted on the MariaDB downloads page next to the file. The second way is to use PGP or GPG to verify the cryptographic signature of the file. These signatures are also posted on the MariaDB downloads page.

After the installation

After installing MariaDB, we can quickly verify that MariaDB is up and running by opening a terminal or command-line window and running the following command (on Windows, we can also open the `mysql.exe` client in the `MariaDB` folder):

```
mysql -u root -p
```

This command connects to MariaDB as the root user (`-u root`) and prompts for the password of that user (`-p`). When prompted, we will type in the password we configured during installation. If no password was set during installation, we simply remove the `-p` from the command. Until a password is set, we can connect without a password.

> Not having a password for the root user is dangerous! If you did not set one during the installation, be sure to set one immediately after the install, following the instructions in *Chapter 3, Securing MariaDB*.

If MariaDB has been successfully installed and started, we should see something similar to the following screenshot when connecting using the previous command to launch the `mysql` command-line client:

```
 ●  dbart@centos70-x86-64:~                                       ⌄ ⌃ ⊗
[dbart@centos70-x86-64 ~]$ mysql -u root
Welcome to the MariaDB monitor.  Commands end with ; or \g.
Your MariaDB connection id is 3
Server version: 10.1.2-MariaDB-wsrep MariaDB Server, wsrep_25.10.r4123

Copyright (c) 2000, 2014, Oracle, SkySQL Ab and others.

Type 'help;' or '\h' for help. Type '\c' to clear the current input statement.

MariaDB [(none)]> ▮
```

If you get the MariaDB command-line prompt, as illustrated in the preceding screenshot, congratulations! You've just installed MariaDB and can successfully connect to the server using the command-line client. You can quit the command-line client for now. Don't worry; we'll come back to it soon.

Troubleshooting installation issues

The MariaDB installers work very well, and they are tested and retested constantly. Occasionally, issues with either installing MariaDB or running it for the first time are discovered, but they are almost always fixed promptly so that users are not affected.

If we do happen to run into an issue when trying to start MariaDB, what should we do?

The first thing we should do is look in the error log. The MariaDB error log is either stored with the system log files (for example, under /var/log/ on Linux) or in the MariaDB data directory. Common locations for the MariaDB data directory include /var/lib/mysql/ on Linux, C:\Program Files\MariaDB <version>\data\ on Windows (<version> is the version number of MariaDB we are using), and /usr/local/var/mysql/ on Mac OS X. The error log file itself will either be called mysql.err or hostname.err where "hostname" is the name that we've given our computer. It is also worth noting that the name and location of the log file can be customized by either the my.cnf file or the my.ini file. *Chapter 2, Configuring MariaDB*, will delve further into this file and its location.

Each entry inside the error log file consists of a timestamp and a description of what went wrong at that timestamp. Sometimes, the information given is enough for us to figure it out ourselves, but at other times, we may need to ask for help. We shouldn't feel bad if we can't figure out an error; even experts are sometimes stumped! If we do need to ask for help, the resources listed on the following link, especially the Maria discuss mailing list and the official IRC channel can help greatly:

https://mariadb.com/kb/en/mariadb/where-are-other-users-and-developers-of-mariadb/

Summary

In this chapter, we installed MariaDB on various operating systems. Our next task is to configure it, which also happens to be the subject and the title of the next chapter.

2
Configuring MariaDB

MariaDB is installed with a generic configuration that is suitable for general use. This is perfect for giving MariaDB a try but might not be suitable for a production database application under a heavy load. There are thousands of ways to tweak the settings to get MariaDB to perform just the way we need it to. Many books have been written on this subject. In this chapter, we'll cover enough of the basics so that we can comfortably edit the MariaDB configuration files and know our way around. Think of this chapter as a MariaDB configuration highlights tour.

The topics that we will cover in this chapter include the following:

- The MariaDB filesystem layout
- Modular configuration on Linux
- The anatomy of the MariaDB configuration file
- Activating configuration changes

The MariaDB filesystem layout

A MariaDB installation is not a single file or even a single directory, so the first stop on our tour is a high-level overview of the filesystem layout. We'll start with Windows and then move on to Linux.

The MariaDB filesystem layout on Windows

On Windows, MariaDB is installed under a directory named with the following pattern:

```
C:\Program Files\MariaDB <major>.<minor>\
```

In the preceding command, `<major>` and `<minor>` refer to the first and second number in the MariaDB version string. So for MariaDB 10.1, the location would be:

```
C:\Program Files\MariaDB 10.1\
```

The only alteration to this location, unless we change it during the installation, is when the 32-bit version of MariaDB is installed on a 64-bit version of Windows. In that case, the default MariaDB directory is at the following location:

```
C:\Program Files x86\MariaDB <major>.<minor>\
```

Under the MariaDB directory on Windows, there are four primary directories: `bin\`, `data\`, `lib\`, and `include\`. There are also several configuration examples and other files under the MariaDB directory and a couple of additional directories (`docs\` and `Share\`), but we won't go into their details here.

The `bin\` directory is where the executable files of MariaDB are located.

The `data\` directory is where databases are stored; it is also where the primary MariaDB configuration file, `my.ini`, is stored. We'll talk about this file later in the section *The anatomy of the MariaDB configuration file*.

The `lib\` directory contains various library and plugin files.

Lastly, the `include\` directory contains files that are useful for application developers.

We don't generally need to worry about the `bin\`, `lib\`, and `include\` directories; it's enough for us to be aware that they exist and know what they contain. The `data\` directory is where we'll spend most of our time in this chapter, and when using MariaDB.

Feel free to read the next two sections, which explain the location of MariaDB files on Linux systems, or jump ahead to the section *The anatomy of the MariaDB configuration file*.

The MariaDB filesystem layout on Linux

On Linux distributions, MariaDB follows the default filesystem layout. Feel free to skip this section if you are working with Windows.

For example, the MariaDB binaries are placed under `/usr/bin/`, libraries are placed under `/usr/lib/`, manual pages are placed under `/usr/share/man/`, and so on.

However, there are some key MariaDB-specific directories and file locations that we should know about. Two of them are locations that are the same across most Linux distributions. These locations are the `/usr/share/mysql/` and `/var/lib/mysql/` directories.

The `/usr/share/mysql/` directory contains helper scripts that are used during the initial installation of MariaDB, translations (so we can have error and system messages in different languages), and character set information. We don't need to worry about these files and scripts; it's enough to know that this directory exists and contains important files.

The `/var/lib/mysql/` directory is the default location for our actual database data and the related files such as logs. There is not much need to worry about this directory as MariaDB will handle its contents automatically; for now, it's enough to know that it exists.

The next directory we should know about is the one where the MariaDB plugins are stored. Unlike the previous two, the location of this directory varies. On Debian and Ubuntu systems, this directory is at the following location:

`/usr/lib/mysql/plugin/`

In distributions such as Fedora, Red Hat, and CentOS, the location of the plugin directory varies depending on whether our system is 32 bit or 64 bit. If unsure, we can just look in both. The possible locations are:

`/lib64/mysql/plugin/`

`/lib/mysql/plugin/`

The basic rule of thumb is that if we don't have a `/lib64/` directory, we have a 32-bit version of Fedora, Red Hat, or CentOS installed.

As with `/usr/share/mysql/`, we don't need to worry about the contents of the MariaDB plugin directory. It's enough to know that it exists and contains important files. Also, if in the future we install a new MariaDB plugin, this directory is where it will go.

The last directory that we should know about is only found on Debian and the distributions based on Debian such as Ubuntu. Its location is as follows:

`/etc/mysql/`

The `/etc/mysql/` directory is where the configuration information for MariaDB is stored; specifically, it is stored in the following two locations:

`/etc/mysql/my.cnf`

`/etc/mysql/conf.d/`

There are additional files in the directory, but we can safely ignore them for now. We'll look into the contents of the `my.cnf` file in the section *The anatomy of the MariaDB configuration file*, and we'll talk about the special `/etc/mysql/conf.d/` directory in the *Modular configuration on Linux* section.

Fedora, Red Hat, CentOS, and related systems don't have an `/etc/mysql/` directory by default, but they do have a `my.cnf` file and a directory that serves the same purpose that the `/etc/mysql/conf.d/` directory does on Debian and Ubuntu. They are at the following two locations:

`/etc/my.cnf`

`/etc/my.cnf.d/`

The `my.cnf` files, regardless of location, function the same on all Linux versions and on Windows, where it is often named `my.ini`. The `/etc/my.cnf.d/` and `/etc/mysql/conf.d/` directories, as mentioned, serve the same purpose. We'll spend the next section going over these two directories.

Modular configuration on Linux

The `/etc/my.cnf.d/` and `/etc/mysql/conf.d/` directories are special locations for the MariaDB configuration files. They are found on the MariaDB releases for Linux such as Debian, Ubuntu, Fedora, Red Hat, and CentOS.

We will only have one or the other of them, never both, and regardless of which one we have, their function is the same. The basic idea behind these directories is to allow the package manager (APT or YUM) to be able to install packages for MariaDB, which include additions to MariaDB's configuration without needing to edit or change the main `my.cnf` configuration file. It's easy to imagine the harm that would be caused if we installed a new plugin package and it overwrote a carefully crafted and tuned configuration file. With these special directories, the package manager can simply add a file to the appropriate directory and be done.

When the MariaDB server and the clients and utilities included with MariaDB start up, they first read the main `my.cnf` file and then any files that they find under the `/etc/my.cnf.d/` or `/etc/mysql/conf.d/` directories that have the extension `.cnf` because of a line at the end of the default configuration files. For example, MariaDB includes a plugin called feedback whose sole purpose is to send back anonymous statistical information to the MariaDB developers. They use this information to help guide future development efforts. It is disabled by default but can easily be enabled by adding `feedback=on` to a `[mysqld]` group of the MariaDB configuration file (we'll talk about configuration groups in the following section). We could add the required lines to our main `my.cnf` file or, better yet, we can create a file called `feedback.cnf` (MariaDB doesn't care what the actual filename is, apart from the `.cnf` extension) with the following content:

`[mysqld]`

`feedback=on`

All we have to do is put our `feedback.cnf` file in the `/etc/my.cnf.d/` or `/etc/mysql/conf.d/` directory and when we start or restart the server, the `feedback.cnf` file will be read and the plugin will be turned on. Doing this for a single plugin on a solitary MariaDB server may seem like too much work, but suppose we have 100 servers, and if we further assume that since the servers are doing different things, each of them has a slightly different `my.cnf` configuration file. Without using our small `feedback.cnf` file to turn on the feedback plugin on all of them, we would have to connect to each server in turn and manually add `feedback=on` to the `[mysqld]` group of the file. This would get tiresome and there is also a chance that we might make a mistake with one or several of the files that we edit, even if we try to automate the editing in some way. Copying a single file to each server that only does one thing (turning on the feedback plugin in our example) is much faster and much safer. And, if we have an automated deployment system in place, copying the file to every server can be almost instant.

> Caution! Because the configuration settings in the `/etc/my.cnf.d/` or `/etc/mysql/conf.d/` directory are read after the settings in the `my.cnf` file, they can override or change the settings in our main `my.cnf` file. This can be a good thing if that is what we want and expect. Conversely, it can be a bad thing if we are not expecting that behavior.

The anatomy of the MariaDB configuration file

Looking at the contents of the MariaDB configuration file for the first time can be a scary experience, but it doesn't have to be. It's actually laid out quite logically. Sometimes, the hardest part is just knowing where it is. We'll review that first, and then go into the various parts that make up the file.

The configuration file is just a text file and we can edit it with our favorite text editor. Even though the extensions may be different (`.ini` or `.cnf`), the contents of the files are the same. Apart from empty lines, which can be ignored, there are four main types of entries in a MariaDB configuration file. These are: comments, groups, options with no values, and options with values. We'll discuss each of them in turn.

Where is my configuration file?

This may seem like a question that should have only one answer, but in an effort to be flexible, MariaDB looks for the `my.cnf` or the `my.ini` configuration file in several different locations.

As mentioned previously, on Windows, the MariaDB configuration file is named `my.ini` by default and is found in the data directory (see the section The *MariaDB filesystem layout on Windows* to learn where the data directory is located on Windows). The file can also be named `my.cnf`, just as it is in Linux, and MariaDB will also look in the following additional locations for it:

```
C:\WINDOWS\my.ini
```

```
C:\WINDOWS\my.cnf
```

```
C:\my.ini
```

```
C:\my.cnf
```

On Linux, the MariaDB configuration file is always named `my.cnf` and is almost always found at one of the following two locations:

```
/etc/my.cnf
```

```
/etc/mysql/my.cnf
```

MariaDB will look for the file at both locations, but if the files exist at both locations, the options in the file that MariaDB reads last will override the options that it read in the first file. So, to avoid confusion, we should only have one or the other and if we discover we have both for some reason, we should combine them into one file.

Comments

Comment lines are lines that begin with # (the hash character) or ; (a semicolon). Comments are ignored by MariaDB. They often contain useful information and are a great place to keep notes when we make changes to the file. Comments can also start in the middle of the line. Just think of anything from the initial comment character to the end of a line as a comment. Here are some examples:

```
# Here is a comment
; This is also a comment
port = 3306 # This is a comment about the 'port' option
```

Groups

Groups are sections or parts in a configuration file. A typical MariaDB installation is composed of a server program, one or more client programs, and several utility programs. Each of these have their own individual configuration options and they can all be set in our `my.cnf` or `my.ini` file. Even the individual series of MariaDB have their own group identifiers (these are useful if we are testing a development version and want to enable a new feature without affecting older servers that use the same configuration file).

A group begins with a name enclosed in square brackets ([]) on a line, by itself. The group continues to the end of the file or to the beginning of the next group, whichever comes first. The following is an example of the often used `mysqld` group:

```
[mysqld]
# Configuration options for the mysqld program go here
```

Incidentally, `mysqld` is the name of the MariaDB server program binary. The group is named after the binary's file name. In addition to `[mysqld]`, other common groups include the following:

```
[server]
  # the same as [mysqld]
[mysql]
  # configuration options for the mysql command-line client
[client]
  # the same as [mysql]
[client-server]
  # configuration options for both clients and the server
[mysqladmin]
  # configuration options for the mysqladmin program
[mysqlcheck]
  # configuration options for the mysqlcheck utility
[mariadb-10.1]
  # configuration options just for MariaDB 10.1 series servers
```

There are many other possible groups, but these are enough to get the idea. We just use the ones we want and can ignore the others.

In each group, we set options. There are two types, those which don't require a corresponding value and those that do.

Options that do not require values

Configuration options either take a value or not. Those that do not need a value appear on a line by themselves with no equals sign (=). They are used for options that are either on or off, so there is no need for arguments. If it exists in the configuration file (and isn't commented out), the feature is considered on. If it doesn't exist (or it is commented out), the feature is set to whatever the default is (ON or OFF). An example would be as follows:

```
no-auto-rehash
```

To turn OFF a feature that is ON by default, just add =OFF to it as follows:

```
no-auto-rehash=OFF
```

We can also be more explicit about turning a feature on by appending =ON to an option. It's not necessary, though.

Options that require values

As mentioned in the previous section, some configuration options require a value of some sort to be set. For example, the default [client] section in the Ubuntu version of the MariaDB my.cnf file contains the following two options:

```
port = 3306
socket = /var/run/mysqld/mysqld.sock
```

Setting options such as port or socket, or any other settings that require a value, without giving a value, will cause an error and MariaDB may refuse to start.

> There is a special line at the end of Linux my.cnf files. It begins with an exclamation mark (!) and its purpose is to include the special /etc/mysql/conf.d/ or /etc/my.cnf.d/ directory. Don't change or remove this line!

Option formatting

Option names are not case sensitive and we can vary the number of spaces around the equals (=) sign. We can also choose to use dashes (-) or underscores (_) in the names. For example, the following two options are the same:

```
max_allowed_packet = 1M
MAX-Allowed-Packet    =    1M
```

One exception to this is with options that have values (described in the *Options that require values* section). If the value is a file or location on a case-sensitive filesystem, like those used on Linux, that value will be case sensitive. The option name itself is not case-sensitive, but the value is. For example, the first two of the following three examples work the same but the third one does not (and on Linux, it will almost assuredly not work):

```
socket = /var/run/mysqld/mysqld.sock
SOCKET = /var/run/mysqld/mysqld.sock
socket = /VAR/run/MySQLd/mysqld.sock
```

Even though MariaDB will accept UPPER or mIxEd case, to keep our my.cnf or my.ini file readable, it is best to keep option names lowercase.

Options, options everywhere

Each individual program and utility included with MariaDB has its own set of configuration options. Run one from the command line with --help and we'll get a list of all the options that the program has and what they are currently set to.

Run the command with --print-defaults and we'll see the values that we've set.

For example, here's the output of mysql --print-defaults on my local machine:

```
shell> mysql --print-defaults


mysql would have been started with the following arguments:


--port=3306 --socket=/var/run/mysqld/mysqld.sock
```

Another method to view what the variables are set to is to use the SHOW VARIABLES and SHOW STATUS commands when connected to MariaDB using the mysql client program. More information on these two commands is available in the MariaDB Knowledge Base at the following links:

- https://mariadb.com/kb/en/mariadb/show-status/
- https://mariadb.com/kb/en/mariadb/show-variables/

If we want to see all the default values for a command (what they would be if we didn't have a config file), use --no-defaults --help –verbose, as follows:

```
shell> mysqld --no-defaults --help –verbose
```

The list that gets printed by the preceding command is quite long, so we won't show it here. And it shows more information than just the default values of the options. The actual variables and options we're interested in are in a table towards the end of the output that begins with the following:

```
Variables (--variable-name=value)
and boolean options {FALSE|TRUE}
```

Putting all of the above information into practice, I've created a fairly generic and heavily commented example my.cnf file. It is available in the code bundle given away with this book.

There isn't space here to go into detail on the many options available for configuring MariaDB. If you want to learn more, a good place to start is in the *Optimization and Tuning* section of the MariaDB Knowledge Base, which is available from:

```
https://mariadb.com/kb/en/optimization-and-tuning/
```

Downloading the example code

You can download the example code files from your account at `http://www.packtpub.com` for all the Packt Publishing books you have purchased. If you purchased this book elsewhere, you can visit `http://www.packtpub.com/support` and register to have the files e-mailed directly to you.

Activating configuration changes

The last stop on our highlights tour of MariaDB configuration is how to activate the changes, once we've made them. To do so, we need to reload or restart MariaDB.

In Windows, we perform the following commands to stop and start MariaDB, respectively:

```
sc stop mysql
sc start mysql
```

The preceding two commands assume that we set the service name to `mysql` (the default) during installation. If we set it to a different name, such as `mariadb`, we would specify that instead.

On Linux systems, the way to activate configuration changes is to reload MariaDB. Traditionally, this is done by doing the following (and we may need to preface it with `sudo`):

```
/etc/init.d/mysql reload
```

However, on some systems, the preferred way to reload MariaDB is as follows:

```
service mysql reload
```

One or the other, and possibly both, will work.

We can also use the SET command to temporarily set the options. See the MariaDB Knowledge Base for more information on using this command from:

```
https://mariadb.com/kb/en/mariadb/set/
```

Example my.cnf file

There's an awful lot of information in this chapter about file locations, comments, options, groups, and so on. If you're anything like me, your head is probably swimming, wondering how you're ever going to make sense of it all. To see the big picture view of how everything works together, I've created an example my.cnf file with lots of comments to explain the different parts and settings of a typical my.cnf file. You can download it from the book's website.

Summary

That's it for our configuration highlights tour! We've learned where the various bits and pieces of MariaDB are installed and about the different parts that make up a typical MariaDB configuration file.

The next chapter is on securing MariaDB. After all, now that we know how MariaDB is configured, we wouldn't want some nefarious character to mess things up, would we? We'll cover an easy way to secure our new installation of MariaDB, and go over the basic things that we can do to keep our database secure.

3
Securing MariaDB

Bad things happen, whether accidentally or on purpose, and we want to protect our MariaDB database against both. Threats come in many different forms and come from many different places, including—but not limited to—physical threats, filesystem threats, network threats, and user threats.

The topics that we will cover in this chapter include the following:

- Security layers
- Securing MariaDB in 10 seconds
- Connecting safely
- Server security
- Building security
- Internal network security
- Internet security

Security layers

You can think of the data in your database as being at the center of a set of rings, as illustrated by the following figure:

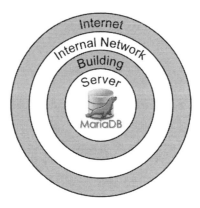

The outermost ring is the **Internet**. This is the outside world. If we are running a business, this is where our customers are. It's also where many attacks originate.

The next two rings are our **Internal Network** and the **Building** where our MariaDB database server is located. Internal corporate networks can span several buildings, but if we're a small business or a hobbyist, the network might just be a single building or even a room or two inside a building or a house. We need to be as careful regarding the security on our internal network as we are on the external Internet, especially seeing as more attacks come from inside networks than from the outside world.

Physical security is also important. If an attacker can simply walk in and take the server or computer where our MariaDB database is present and walk out with it, none of our network and other security measures will mean anything. It's trivial for an attacker to gain access to our data if they have physical access to the machine.

The next ring is the **Server** on which MariaDB is running. Questions that we should ask about security on the server include things like, "who can log in?", "where can they log in from?", "who has the administrative rights?", "does it have monitoring and backup systems in place so that we can keep an eye on it?" The answers to all of these questions depend on factors that are beyond the scope of this book, but we should try to find out the answers.

For example, if you know that only three other people have login access to the server, we could tighten up security to a level—such as requiring SSH keys to login—that might be unacceptable on a server that has hundreds of users or is shared with other departments. Knowing who the administrators of the server are is useful because we want to know who to call if something goes wrong. It's the same for the backup and monitoring systems; we need to know where they are and how to access them because if we don't, they won't be of much use to us when a problem occurs.

Now we're inside the server and have come to the center of the rings—the MariaDB database itself. If it looks like MariaDB is sitting right at the center of a bullseye, that's because it is. Security starts here and there's no better time to secure our MariaDB installation than right now. We'll begin by working our way from the inside out.

Securing MariaDB in 10 seconds

The first thing that we need to do after installing MariaDB is to run the `mysql_secure_installation` script. This useful tool is included with MariaDB, and it's found among the other tools and binaries that ship with MariaDB. Its sole purpose is to quickly and easily set up some basic security. To run it, open a command line and enter the following command:

```
mysql_secure_installation
```

The script will ask several questions. For nearly all of them, it's best to answer yes (y). The only question that we might want to answer no (n) to is when the script asks us to set a root user password. If we've already set a root password, we can safely skip this question (the script is helpful enough to tell us when it is safe to say no).

The other questions include removing the test database, removing the default anonymous user, and disallowing remote root user logins. The anonymous user and test database are included in the default MariaDB installation for testing purposes, but there's almost never a reason to keep them. We can always create a new test user and database, or several, for our testing needs.

The following is the output of a complete run of the script on a server running
Ubuntu 14.04:

```
shell> mysql_secure_installation


NOTE: RUNNING ALL PARTS OF THIS SCRIPT IS RECOMMENDED FOR ALL
      MariaDB SERVERS IN PRODUCTION USE!  PLEASE READ EACH
      STEP CAREFULLY!




In order to log into MariaDB to secure it, we'll need the
current password for the root user.  If you've just
installed MariaDB, and you haven't set the root password
yet, the password will be blank, so you should just press
enter here.


Enter current password for root (enter for none):
OK, successfully used password, moving on...


Setting the root password ensures that nobody can log into
the MariaDB root user without proper authorization.


Set root password? [Y/n] y
New password:
Re-enter new password:


Password updated successfully!
Reloading privilege tables.
 ... Success!


By default, a MariaDB installation has an anonymous user,
allowing anyone to log into MariaDB without the need to have
a user account created for them.  This is intended only for
testing, and to make the installation go a bit smoother.
You should remove them before moving into a production
environment.


Remove anonymous users? [Y/n] y
```

```
... Success!


Normally, root should only be allowed to connect from the
'localhost'. This ensures that nobody is able to guess the root
password from the network.

Disallow root login remotely? [Y/n] y
 ... Success!


By default, MariaDB comes with a database named 'test' that
anyone can access. This is also intended only for testing,
and should be removed before moving into a production environment.

Remove test database and access to it? [Y/n] y


 - Dropping test database...
 ... Success!
 - Removing privileges on test database...
 ... Success!


Reloading the privilege tables will ensure that all changes
made so far will take effect immediately.


Reload privilege tables now? [Y/n] y
 ... Success!


Cleaning up...


All done!  If you've completed all of the above steps, your
MariaDB installation should now be secure.


Thanks for using MariaDB!
```

As the output of the script says, after running it, our MariaDB installation is now secure. In fact, if we run it immediately after installing MariaDB, the only user that will now be able to connect is the root user, and it will only be able to do so while logged in to or sitting in front of the actual computer that MariaDB is running on. This isn't very convenient and we don't want to give other users or applications the root user password, so we'll eventually have to add users and open things up at least a little; *Chapter 4, Administering MariaDB*, goes into this subject.

Connecting safely

Now that the root user has a password, it's up to us to make sure that password, and the passwords of all the other users we will inevitably create, stay secure and not get revealed by mistake. One of the most important ways to do that is to always follow good practice when connecting.

Connecting safely on the command line

When connecting to MariaDB as the root, or any other user from the command line, we tell the `mysql` command-line client that we are connecting with a password by using the `-p` flag. When we do so, we can either specify the password right after the `-p` flag with no space in between, as shown in the following example:

```
mysql -u root -pmypassword
```

Or, even better, we can just leave the `-p` flag by itself and the client will prompt us for the password, as shown in the following example:

```
mysql -u root -p
Enter password:
```

It is almost never a good idea to have our password visible on the command line as in the first example. The reason is that the status and system logs may record the command. This is very useful in determining who is connecting and when, but it is very dangerous as it exposes the password to anyone who can access the logs. By using just `-p` and then entering the password when prompted, the password is not echoed to the screen and is not logged or displayed.

Connecting safely in scripts

A situation might arise where we want to create a script that connects to our MariaDB database at certain times, in order to do housekeeping or other useful tasks. Our script will connect to MariaDB using a database user and, naturally, we want this user to have rights to only do the things that he/she needs to do, and to have a good password as well. Using the password prompt method will work if we use a tool such as expect on Linux or Mac OS, but that may not be available or work in all cases, such as if we are on Windows or cannot install expect. So how do we connect without exposing the password? The answer is option files.

Option files are just text files, and technically we can create one anywhere, but it should preferably be in a logical location, such as in the same folder that the script is in or in a hidden directory in our `home` directory.

The contents of the option file can be any of the options that we can put into a `my.cnf` file, but for the preceding example of supplying a script with a username and password, the contents are very simple, and only three lines — the first starting a client section and the other two specifying the username and the password to use (`scriptuser` and `scriptpassword` in this example):

```
[client]
user = scriptuser
password=scriptpassword
```

Notice that the preceding example uses spaces around the equals sign on the user line, but not on the password line. This is because passwords can have spaces in them, so the MariaDB `mysql` command-line client starts reading the password immediately after the equals sign. So, unless the first character of our password is a space, we start the password immediately after the equals sign.

In our script, all we need to do is tell the client to read the file by using the `--defaults-file` option, as follows:

```
mysql --defaults-file=/path/to/my-file
```

With the preceding command in place, the client will read the file as it connects and use the username and password that we supplied (along with any other client options that we add in the file).

To be safe while using this method, we should set the file such that it is readable only by the user who runs the script. We can consult our operating system documentation for the specifics on how to do this. On Linux and Mac OS systems, a good command to use is the following one:

```
chmod 600 my-file
```

The preceding command sets the file as readable and writable by the user who owns the file (6) and no access for everyone else (the two zeroes). Consult the `chmod` documentation for full details regarding this.

On Windows, we can accomplish the same thing by right-clicking on the file in the file manager, selecting **Properties** and then adjusting the access permissions. Consult the Windows documentation for full instructions.

Server security

With MariaDB itself locked down nice and tight, and by using good password practices, we now need to look at the computer that MariaDB is running on.

If we are running MariaDB on our own desktop or laptop, and we are the only one who can log into it, then there's not much to worry about apart from the normal things we do to keep our computer secure, such as virus and malware protection, system updates, keeping it in a secure location, and so on. It is also useful to encrypt our hard drives, or at least our home folders, using an operation supported by most modern operating systems.

When we install MariaDB on a dedicated server then there is more that we have to worry about. Servers are almost always multiuser, so as part of server security, we need to know who can log in and most importantly, who has root or administrator access. If we are the administrator of the machine, we can ensure that only those we want to have access to the administrator or root have access. If we're using MariaDB on a machine that our IT department gave us access to, then we need to find out who has access and what their rights are, so that we know who has sufficient rights on the server to make any changes, including those that could be harmful.

Building security

We come to building security by continuing out to the next ring. All the protection inside the server won't do us any good if the server decides to take a walk at three in the morning. Just as we secure the inside of the server, we need to secure the outside too.

Firstly, where is the server located? Is it in a common area where anyone in the office could get to it? This could be bad on a number of levels, the first being that someone could accidentally or on purpose disconnect the power supply to it. We can mitigate external power outages to some extent by installing battery backup units and such, but someone with physical access to the machine can easily get around that and cut the power supply to our servers. To its credit, MariaDB — when we use a transactional or crash safe storage engine—guards against losing or corrupting data in such cases, but at the very least, a surprise power outage will disrupt every application that needs to talk to that database server. If the server is in a locked room, we should find out who has access to the room.

Also consider the building. Most businesses and offices close at night—the building or office is locked at closing time and opens again in the morning—however, this is not true for all businesses. For example, what if the server is located in the manager's office of a 24-hour supermarket and the door to that office is always open or unlocked? If so, then we need to think about locking that door (automatically if people keep forgetting to lock it), or getting a small lockable server cage installed which is bolted to the wall or floor, or come up with some other way of securing the server.

An easy analogy is to treat a server like money. We use database servers to either save money, generate income, or both. If we would feel comfortable leaving a large stack of money in the location our server is in, then it is probably a pretty good place for our server (assuming there is power and adequate cooling).

The best place for a server is usually with other servers in a dedicated server room. Preferably, this should be a room that is secure and where access is controlled with well-defined security policies and procedures. These could range from a locked closet (that only a few chosen people can access and which has a server sitting on a shelf) to a locked server cage at a large data center (that has raised floor cooling, 24 x 7 on-site security, and everything in surplus). There is no one particular location that is right for every situation, but we need to evaluate ours and make sure that our server is physically protected.

Internal network security

The security of the internal network is related to building security. If our MariaDB server is located in a locked server closet, then we will likely be accessing it remotely from our desk. If so, then we need to at least be aware of the security of our internal network. Some key questions to ask our local network administrator include the following:

- Is there a firewall in place to prevent outside access to our network?
    - If there is, great! If not, suggest that one be added.

- Is there a Wi-Fi network that is directly connected to our internal network, or is the Wi-Fi sectioned off into its own network?
    - If the Wi-Fi network is connected directly to the internal network, see if that can be changed.

- What type of access, if any, do telecommuting employees have — VPN, SSH, or something else?

    ◦ If telecommuting employees are forced into using VPN or SSH to connect, that is good, as both of those access methods are encrypted. If the answer is something else, we need to find out if it is secure and encrypted (if it isn't, we need to complain).

- Are our database users defined with % for the network part or are they all restricted to localhost or known valid locations and networks? The % character is the wildcard character and its presence in the network part of a username means that the user can connect from anywhere, which may be convenient, but is not good from a security standpoint. We'll go into this in more detail in *Chapter 4*, *Administering MariaDB*.

- If we are in a large company, do different departments have their own segregated networks, and if so, do they have access to the network the server is on?

- If our database is a part of a project inside the company for a product in the early stages of development, we might not want the salespeople, for example, finding out about it until it is ready.

- At the very least, when we connect to the server remotely, we must always do so securely using SSH or an encrypted tunnel. And if we don't know how to do so, we need to learn right away.

Internet security

The last ring is the outside world, that is, the Internet. Generally speaking, we don't want to expose our MariaDB database server directly to the Internet ever. It's not that MariaDB is especially vulnerable, any more than any other piece of software, it's just that it's never necessary to expose it to the Internet and part of good security is to not expose something unless we have to (in the same way that a poker player doesn't want to reveal his hand to the other players). When MariaDB is running on a web server, the web server software can connect directly with no need for a network connection. If our MariaDB server is separate from our web server, then we can almost always connect the two of them together over our internal network and, if not, we can set up some sort of secure tunnel between the two.

 If you do think you've found a legitimate reason to expose your MariaDB server to the entire Internet, I strongly encourage you to talk with one of the many fine MariaDB consulting companies and have them help you work out an alternative solution.

Summary

In this chapter, we learned a bit about securing our MariaDB server. Security is a big topic and cannot possibly be covered completely in a single chapter, and there are many resources, both online and offline, to help you learn more about this important topic. But don't limit yourself to books or articles about securing MariaDB or other databases; also take the time to learn about system, network, and physical security.

That said, the most secure safe in the world may be one with no doors, windows, or other openings of any kind, but it's not very useful or safe if we can't access it when we need to. So in *Chapter 4*, *Administering MariaDB*, we'll make our currently secure MariaDB server a bit more useful by adding user accounts and learning how to manage them.

4
Administering MariaDB

The root user in our MariaDB database server will have rights to every database and table. We don't want to use the MariaDB root user for day-to-day operations or hand out the password to anyone who doesn't absolutely need to have it. Instead, we want to create users that have specific rights to the specific databases they need to work with.

In this chapter, we will cover the following topics:

- User privileges
- Creating users
- Granting, revoking, and showing permissions
- Setting and changing passwords
- Removing users

User privileges

The privileges or rights that we can grant to users are many and varied. They break down into three main categories:

- Global administrative user privileges
- Database, table, and column user privileges
- Miscellaneous user privileges and limits

when you look through the following tables of privileges, don't worry if you do not understand every privilege and what it means. For now, it's enough to just be aware of them and of the fact that privileges are how MariaDB controls what a user can do.

Global administrative user privileges

The following table lists the global administrative user privileges. Global privileges apply to all databases, and tables within those databases, which belong to an entire MariaDB database server or server cluster:

Privilege	Description
CREATE USER	The ability to create a user using the CREATE USER statement.
FILE	The ability to use the LOAD DATA INFILE statement and the LOAD_FILE() function.
PROCESS	The ability to use the SHOW PROCESSLIST command.
RELOAD	The ability to use the FLUSH statement.
REPLICATION CLIENT	The ability to use the SHOW MASTER STATUS and SHOW SLAVE STATUS commands.
REPLICATION SLAVE	The ability to get updates made on the replication master server.
SHOW DATABASES	The ability to list all the databases on the server.
SHUTDOWN	The ability to shut down the server using the mysqladmin shutdown command.
SUPER	The ability to use superuser statements such as CHANGE MASTER TO..., PURGE LOGS; to SET global variables; and to KILL other users' threads. This privilege also lets a user connect to the database server even when the maximum configured number of allowed connections (set using the max_connections variable) are being used.

Database, table, and column user privileges

The following table lists the database and table privileges. These privileges apply only to a specific database or a table within a database:

Privilege	Description
ALTER	The ability to change indexes and tables
ALTER ROUTINE	The ability to change or delete procedures and stored functions
CREATE	The ability to create databases and tables
CREATE ROUTINE	The ability to create procedures and stored functions
CREATE TEMPORARY TABLES	The ability to create temporary tables

Privilege	Description
CREATE VIEW	The ability to create views
DELETE	The ability to delete entries (rows) from tables
DROP	The ability to delete entire databases and tables
EVENT	The ability to alter, create, and drop events from the event scheduler
EXECUTE	The ability to execute stored functions and procedures
INDEX	The ability to create or delete indexes
INSERT	The ability to insert new rows of data into a table
LOCK TABLES	The ability to lock and unlock tables
SELECT	The ability to read data from a table
SHOW VIEW	The ability to use the SHOW CREATE VIEW statement
TRIGGER	The ability to use the CREATE TRIGGER and DROP TRIGGER statements
UPDATE	The ability to modify rows in a table

Miscellaneous user privileges and limits

The following table lists the miscellaneous privileges that don't quite fit into either of the two previous categories:

Privilege	Description
ALL PRIVILEGES	This can be used to grant all available privileges to a user. It does not grant the GRANT OPTION privilege, and can be shortened to ALL.
GRANT OPTION	This gives a user the ability to grant other users the privileges they have. This is given at the end of the GRANT statement. See the *Granting Permissions* section of this chapter from some examples.

There are also several limits that we can place on user accounts. These are given in the following table:

Limit	Description
MAX_QUERIES_PER_HOUR	This is the number of SQL statements or queries that the user account can issue per hour. This includes updates.
MAX_UPDATES_PER_HOUR	This is the number of SQL update statements (not queries) that the user account can issue per hour.
MAX_CONNECTIONS_PER_HOUR	This is the number of connections that the user account can start per hour.
MAX_USER_CONNECTIONS	This is the number of simultaneous connections to the database server that the user account can have. If set to zero, the number will be equal to the max_connections setting. If the max_connections setting is also zero, then there is no limit to the number of simultaneous connections the user account can have.

Full documentation of the various privileges can be found at the following location:
https://mariadb.com/kb/en/grant/

Creating users

Creating a user in MariaDB involves a two-step process. First, we create the user using the CREATE USER statement, and then we give or GRANT the user the privileges that we want them to have. We'll go over the CREATE USER statement in this section and the GRANT statement in the granting, revoking, and showing permissions section.

A CREATE USER statement has the following pattern:

```
CREATE USER 'username'@'host' IDENTIFIED BY 'password';
```

We customize the username, host, and password parts to the appropriate values. If we don't want to specify a password (though this is not recommended!) then we can drop the IDENTIFIED BY 'password' part. This, and all the other SQL statements that we input into MariaDB, need to end with a semicolon (;).

The host part can be several things. It can be the hostname of the computer which the user connects from, the IP address of the computer that the user connects from, the network that the user connects from, or it can be the wildcard symbol %, which means any host.

Let's take a look at some examples. In the first example, the user can login from anywhere because of the wildcard character, %, in the host part. The user's password is bomber.

```
CREATE USER 'boyd'@'%' IDENTIFIED BY 'bomber';
```

The following three examples demonstrate the use of various host names. The first specifies the localhost, which means the local server on which MariaDB is running. The next example specifies a single specific host, and the third uses % to specify any subdomain of the example.net domain.

```
CREATE USER 'tom'@'localhost' IDENTIFIED BY 'retail';
CREATE USER 'richard'@'powr.example.net' IDENTIFIED BY 'nuclear';
CREATE USER 'robert'@'%.example.net' IDENTIFIED BY 'pilot';
```

Instead of hostnames, we can also use IP addresses as shown in the following three examples. The first has an exact IP address identifying a single computer, and the second uses a % sign in the last quad of the IP address so that any computer where the first three sets of numbers in the IP address match will be able to connect. The third uses a subnet mask, but the end result (in this example at least) is the same as the second.

```
CREATE USER 'dallin'@'192.168.1.1' IDENTIFIED BY 'judge';
CREATE USER 'russell'@'192.168.1.%' IDENTIFIED BY 'surgeon';
CREATE USER 'russell'@'192.168.1.0/255.255.255.0' IDENTIFIED BY
'business';
```

One benefit of using IP addresses instead of domain names is that no name resolution or domain validation needs to be made. Such system calls used to look up and check the validity of domains can be costly if they are happening many times per second and might take time and resources better spent on other things. To enforce a no-domain-names policy, add skip-name-resolv=1 to the [mysqld] section of the my.cnf or my.ini file.

Complete documentation of the CREATE USER statement is available at the following location:

https://mariadb.com/kb/en/create-user/

Granting, revoking, and showing permissions

By default, new users do not have the permission to do anything except logging in, which is not very useful. So the next thing we need to do is give them the permissions that they need. Over time, we may need to remove or revoke the privileges we gave them earlier, and from time to time we'll want to look up a user to see what privileges they have.

Granting permissions

This is done using the GRANT statement. Using this statement, we will be able to GRANT users the appropriate permissions. GRANT statements have the following basic pattern:

```
GRANT <privileges> ON <database> TO <user>;
```

We customize the `<privileges>`, `<database>`, and `<user>` parts as needed. The `<user>` section should match the `'username'@'host'` part of the CREATE statement. Otherwise, we'll be creating a new user. We can also add an IDENTIFIED BY `'password'` section to the end of the GRANT statement if we want to change the password of the user (or add a password to a user that doesn't have one).

The following are some examples. The first one grants all privileges, including the ability to GRANT privileges to other users, on all databases and the user can log in from anywhere. We should not often set up users with such broad authority, but when we do, we need to make sure that we use an appropriate CREATE USER statement first and assign the user a password (or assign the password here).

> If a user doesn't exist before we use the GRANT statement, the user will be created, but if the user doesn't exist and our GRANT statement doesn't include an IDENTIFIED BY `'password'` section, then the user will be created without a password. So, it's a good habit to first create the user with a password, and then grant the user the rights that they need.

```
GRANT ALL ON *.* TO 'robert'@'%' WITH GRANT OPTION;
```

The following example is for a standard set of permissions for a regular user who needs read and write access to a database called serv. If a user just needs read access, we can assign the user the SELECT privilege. By specifying serv.* as the database, the user only has these rights on the tables in the serv database. Multiple privileges are separated by commas.

```
GRANT SELECT,INSERT,UPDATE,DELETE ON serv.* TO 'jeffrey'@'localhost';
```

The following user has read access (SELECT) to just the staff table in the edu database, and the user has the GRANT OPTION privilege so that they can grant that same right to other users.

```
GRANT SELECT ON edu.staff TO 'david'@'localhost' WITH GRANT OPTION;
```

The following example gives a user all rights on the logan database. We'll also limit this user to 100 queries per hour, just because we can. The limit will apply to every database that can be accessed by the quentin user and not just to queries that the user runs on the logan database.

```
GRANT ALL ON logan.* TO 'quentin'@'localhost' WITH
MAX_QUERIES_PER_HOUR 100;
```

 Complete documentation of the GRANT statement is available at the following location:

https://mariadb.com/kb/en/grant/

Revoking permissions

Sometimes it becomes necessary to remove a privilege or two from a user, or to give them more privileges. Giving additional privileges is easy; just run an additional GRANT statement with the new rights and they will be added to the user's set of permissions. To remove privileges, we use the REVOKE statement. It has the following pattern:

```
REVOKE <privileges> ON <database> FROM <user>;
```

To remove a GRANT OPTION privilege, specify it in the <privileges> section along with any other privileges being revoked. Each permission being removed should be separated from the others with a comma (,). The following example removes the DELETE and GRANT OPTION permissions from the todd user:

```
REVOKE DELETE,GRANT OPTION ON cust.* FROM 'todd'@'%';
```

To remove all privileges from a user (`'neil'@'%.example.com'` in this example), we use the following special command:

```
REVOKE ALL,GRANT OPTION FROM 'neil'@'%.example.com';
```

Generally, it is preferred to use the DROP USER statement, described in the *Removing users* section later on in this chapter, instead of removing all privileges from a user as we are doing here. Of course, we need to customize the user part to match the user for whom we are removing privileges. The statement is also special in that it must be used as written even if the user doesn't have the GRANT OPTION privilege. If we remove the GRANT OPTION privilege from it, the statement won't run.

 Complete documentation of the REVOKE statement is available at the following location:
`https://mariadb.com/kb/en/revoke/`

Showing permissions

To show the permissions granted to a user, we use the SHOW GRANTS command. It has the following pattern:

```
SHOW GRANTS FOR <user>;
```

All we have to do is customize the `<user>` part with the information of the user we want to look at. The following is an example of this:

```
SHOW GRANTS FOR 'dieter'@'10.2.200.4';
```

The output of the SHOW GRANTS command is a GRANT statement that encapsulates all of the user's privileges. This is useful if you want to give another user exactly the same privileges. For example, the output of the preceding SHOW GRANTS command might be as follows:

```
+----------------------------------------------------+
| Grants for dieter@10.2.200.4                       |
+----------------------------------------------------+
| GRANT ALL PRIVILEGES ON *.* TO 'dieter'@'10.2.200.4' |
+----------------------------------------------------+
```

We can simply copy the GRANT statement in the output and change the `<user>` part to create a user with the exactly same privileges.

Setting and changing passwords

To change the password of a user or to set a password for a user that doesn't have one, we can use the GRANT statement, but that implies that we are adding permissions to a user. To change or set a password without changing any permissions; it's much easier to use the SET PASSWORD statement. It has the following pattern:

```
SET PASSWORD FOR <user> = PASSWORD('<password>');
```

The following is an example of this:

```
SET PASSWORD FOR 'henry'@'%' = PASSWORD('niftypassword');
```

 Complete documentation of the SET PASSWORD statement is available at the following location:

https://mariadb.com/kb/en/set-password/

Removing users

In the *Revoking permissions* section given previously in this chapter, there is an example for removing all the privileges of a user, but this doesn't actually remove the user. To remove a user completely, we use the DROP USER statement. It has the following pattern:

```
DROP USER <user>;
```

The following is an example of this:

```
DROP USER 'tom'@'%';
```

When a user is dropped, all permissions are automatically removed as well.

 Complete documentation of the DROP USER statement is available at the following location:

https://mariadb.com/kb/en/drop-user/

Summary

In this chapter, we learned about adding and removing users and giving those users the permissions that they need or taking them away as needed.

Up until now, we've only talked about things related to our databases (securing them, managing users, and so on). We haven't actually done anything with any real data—the stuff that databases are good at storing, manipulating, and retrieving. Well, it is now time to look at this. The next three chapters are all about using MariaDB. We'll learn the basic SQL commands that we can use with the mysql command-line client program to create databases, insert data, read data, and so on in the next three chapters.

5

Using MariaDB – Databases and Tables

From this chapter onwards, we will focus on using the command-line `mysql` client to perform common tasks. In this chapter, you'll learn about the following:

- The `mysql` command-line client application
- Connecting to MariaDB
- Using USE to select a database
- Using SHOW to list all databases on a server
- Creating and deleting databases
- Data, tables, and normalization
- Creating, altering, and dropping tables

The mysql command-line client application

A big part of becoming a MariaDB expert is learning how to effectively and efficiently use the command-line `mysql` client program. Often we will interact with MariaDB using custom programs that have been developed for specific needs. At a lower level though, every interaction that these programs have with MariaDB can be done with the command-line client.

MariaDB has a client-server architecture, which means there are two parts to it—the server, which is the part that does the heavy, behind-the-scenes stuff, and a client, which is the part that we use to access and interact with the server. We hardly ever interact directly with the server part. There are many different clients for MariaDB, but only one is maintained by the MariaDB developers and included with every copy of MariaDB—the `mysql` command-line client.

Connecting to MariaDB

To start the client and connect to MariaDB, we open up a command-line or terminal window and type `mysql` with some options and press *Enter*. The basic syntax is as follows:

```
mysql [-u <username>] [-p] [-h <host>] [<database>]
```

All the options in the previous syntax example are in square brackets (`[]`) to show that they are all optional. The parts in angle brackets (`<>`) are bits that we must supply if we choose to use that option. For example, if we use the -u option, we must supply a username.

Most of the time, we will use the username (`-u`) and password (`-p`) options. We will also often specify the database that we want to connect to when the client launches. When we connect remotely to a MariaDB server on another computer, we will use the host (`-h`) option.

It is possible to add the password after -p on the command line, with a couple of caveats. First, there can't be a space between the -p and the password. For example if our username is tom and our password is `correcthorse` we can use the following command line to log in to MariaDB:

`mysql -u tom -pcorrecthorse`

The second caveat is that doing this is very insecure and should not, in fact, be done. Command-line interpreters and shells are almost always configured to save the commands we run in a history file that could have insecure permissions, meaning that if we make a habit of typing out our password on the command line like this, an attacker only has to gain access to the history file to find out our MariaDB user password.

A successful connection will look similar to the following:

```
daniel@pippin:~$ mysql -u root -p
Enter password:
Welcome to the MariaDB monitor.  Commands end with ; or \g.
```

```
Your MariaDB connection id is 209
Server version: 10.1.2-MariaDB-1~trusty-wsrep-log mariadb.org binary
distribution, wsrep_25.10.r4123


Copyright (c) 2000, 2014, Oracle, SkySQL Ab and others.


Type 'help;' or '\h' for help. Type '\c' to clear the current input
statement.


MariaDB [(none)]>
```

The last line of the output, MariaDB [(none)]>, is the MariaDB prompt. It appears whenever MariaDB is waiting for us to give it a command. Apart from its primary purpose, the prompt gives us two pieces of very useful information. First, the prompt says MariaDB which tells us that we are connecting to an actual MariaDB database server (as opposed to a compatible database server that isn't actually MariaDB). Second, the part in the brackets tells us which database on the server we are currently using by default; in this case, we aren't using any database, so it says (none).

Using USE to select a database

We generally want to be connected to a specific database when we use the command-line client. To use a database, we either specify it on the command line when launching the client as shown in the previous section, or we use the USE command to tell the client which database we want to talk to. The following example illustrates connecting to a database named test. Notice that the prompt changes to let us know the name of the database it is currently connected to.

```
MariaDB [(none)]> USE test;
Reading table information for completion of table and column names
You can turn off this feature to get a quicker startup with -A


Database changed
MariaDB [test]>
```

If the database does not exist when we try to USE it, we will see the following error:

```
MariaDB [(none)]> USE test1;
ERROR 1049 (42000): Unknown database 'test1'
```

Using SHOW to list all databases on a server

To show a list of all of the databases on a server that the current user is allowed to see, use the SHOW DATABASES command as in the following example:

```
MariaDB [(none)]> SHOW DATABASES;
+--------------------+
| Database           |
+--------------------+
| dbt3_s001          |
| flightstats        |
| ham                |
| information_schema |
| isfdb              |
| lds_scriptures     |
| library            |
| mysql              |
| performance_schema |
| test               |
| wikidb             |
+--------------------+
11 rows in set (0.00 sec)


MariaDB [(none)]>
```

The preceding example is from my personal install of MariaDB; the databases listed when you run the command will almost assuredly be different. This command is useful especially if you're given access to an existing MariaDB database server and want to see what databases are available to you, or if you can't quite remember what a specific database was named.

You may have noticed in the previous examples that all the commands ended with a semi-colon (;). This is called the *delimiter* and it is a characteristic feature of **Structured Query Language (SQL)**. We can interact with the command-line client using this language. In basic terms, SQL is a computer language optimized for interacting with a database. MariaDB uses its own variant of SQL which is similar to, but not exactly the same as, the SQL variants used by other databases. When we learn how to write the SQL statements for MariaDB, we also learn a good deal about writing SQL for other databases, but there are some differences. For instance, USE and SHOW are commands which exist in MariaDB, but not in some other database servers that use their own variant of SQL.

Creating and deleting databases

When we install MariaDB, we're installing a database server, not a specific database, and a single MariaDB database server can have several databases inside it. Here's an analogy that can help us understand this arrangement: a database can be thought of as a large filing cabinet. The filing cabinet contains a number of drawers and inside each drawer are files with information. In this analogy, the filing cabinet is a database, the drawers are tables within the database, and the files are rows of data within the tables. So what is MariaDB? It's the room the filing cabinet is located in, and it's a large room so we can put many filing cabinets inside it.

When MariaDB is installed, the installer creates a system database that MariaDB uses to keep track of users, databases, and other housekeeping information. The installer also creates a test database for experimentation and learning, and a couple of read-only, semi-virtual databases where MariaDB stores performance and other statistics. We don't want to use the system database as this could mess up the entire server if we made a mistake. We can't put data into the statistics databases, called information_schema and performance_schema, because they are semi-virtual and read only. We can use the test database, but we probably don't want to use it for anything permanent. So one of our first tasks, when we start using MariaDB, is to create at least one database for us to use.

Another word for a database is schema. In some database servers, a schema and a database are not quite the same thing, but in MariaDB they are. So when we see information_schema, this means the information database. We can even use SCHEMA instead of DATABASE when we are using the command-line client. For example: SHOW SCHEMAS instead of SHOW DATABASES. In this book, we'll stick to the name databases.

Generally, databases are created for specific things or specific applications. For example, we could have an accounting database for the finance department, a human resources database for the HR department, and a parts database for the warehouse.

Creating and dropping (deleting) databases are two things that we will do less often than just about anything else when working with MariaDB. There just isn't much call for it in day-to-day work. We generally create a database and then use it as long as it is needed (which could be for years or decades) and then we delete (drop) it. Thankfully, the commands for creating and dropping a database are very simple, so they're easy to remember.

Using CREATE DATABASE to create a database

As mentioned previously, creating a database is not something we will do often. To create a database in MariaDB, we use the CREATE DATABASE command. The basic syntax is as follows:

```
CREATE DATABASE <databasename>;
```

If the database already exists when we try to create it, we will receive an error. We can suppress the error with IF NOT EXISTS.

The following are some examples:

```
CREATE DATABASE my_database;
CREATE DATABASE IF NOT EXISTS my_database;
```

The preceding two commands are equivalent if the database does not exist. If the database does exist, the first command will exit with an error and the second command will do nothing.

 Full documentation of the CREATE DATABASE command is available at the following location:
https://mariadb.com/kb/en/create-database/

Using DROP DATABASE to delete a database

As mentioned before, it isn't often that we need to remove or delete a database, but when we do, we use the DROP DATABASE command. Out of the database commands, this one is by far the easiest, but it is potentially the most dangerous. The basic syntax is as follows:

```
DROP DATABASE <databasename>;
```

If the named database doesn't exist when we try to drop it, we will receive an error. We can suppress the error with `IF EXISTS`.

The following are a couple of examples that drop the database that we just created:

```
DROP DATABASE my_database;
DROP DATABASE IF EXISTS my_database;
```

The preceding two commands are equivalent if the database `my_database` exists. If the database does not exist, the first command will exit with an error and the second command will do nothing.

As mentioned previously, the `DROP DATABASE` command can be very dangerous. Why is this, you might ask? This is because if you have the appropriate permission to drop a database, MariaDB trusts you and will delete the database and everything in it when you tell it to, no questions asked. So when setting up users, it is important to give only trusted users, who actually need it, the ability to use the `DROP DATABASE` command. More on setting up users and giving them permissions is given in *Chapter 4, Administering MariaDB*.

Warning: When dropping a database, user privileges for the database are not removed. We need to revoke them manually, or drop the user entirely; otherwise, if or when the database is recreated, the user will still have the privileges. See *Chapter 4, Administering MariaDB*, for information on managing users and their privileges.

Complete documentation of the `DROP DATABASE` command is available at the following location:

https://mariadb.com/kb/en/drop-database/

Data, tables, and normalization

The primary purpose of a database is to store data. Data is information, usually text-based, but not always, and this data could be anything from a company phone directory, to patient medical information, to an auto parts list, or even reviews of gourmet hot sauces complete with pictures of the bottles.

Database servers such as MariaDB store information, no matter what it is, in a structure called a *table*. Tables are two-dimensional data structures containing rows and columns. A row corresponds to a single record in a database and records are divided into columns. Think of database tables like a specialized spreadsheet.

The columns in a database can have relationships defined in one way or another. For example, the id column in an employee table may relate to the `employee_id` column in an address table. These relationships (also called foreign keys) are why we call MariaDB a relational database server.

A database without tables of data is nothing more than an entry in the MariaDB system database (this database is called `mysql`) and a directory in the file system under the `datadir` directory. Until we create some tables and start adding data to those tables, our new database is useless.

There are few things in MariaDB that we will spend more time on, at least in the beginning, than when we create the tables in our database.

When we create a table, we are defining its structure. This structure includes such things as the number of columns and the type of data that we want to store in each column. Data types include things such as numbers, text, and dates. For example, if we are creating an employee table, we might decide that each row will contain an employee identification number (number), a surname (text), any given names (text), a preferred name (text), a birthdate (date), and so on.

We might also want to store the e-mail addresses, phone numbers, and home addresses of the employees, but we don't necessarily want to store that kind of data in the same table. Why? Because they are things people often have more than one of. For example, many people have both personal and work e-mail addresses. The same holds true for phone numbers and, for some people, even houses. If we try to design a table that has enough fields for the multiples of phone numbers and e-mail addresses that people have, it will quickly become unwieldy with too many columns, and with possibly no single row that uses all of them. Instead, we break apart the data into multiple tables, and define the relationships between the tables.

A good rule of thumb is to break the information apart into a separate table when it is clear there could be multiples of it. For example, it wouldn't make sense to have a single orders table in a company database that contains everything. Instead, we would have a customers table for the core customer information, an addresses table to hold the multiple addresses that the customers might want us to ship items to, an items table for the various things we might ship to a customer, and lastly, an orders table to actually track the orders made by customers. Of course, this is only one way to split the information apart and we might also need to store payment, supplier, and other information.

The process by which we refine our table definitions and split our data off into multiple tables is called normalization. There isn't space here for a complete discussion of this process, but the MariaDB Knowledge Base has a page which discusses it in depth and you can refer to the following location:

```
https://mariadb.com/kb/en/recap-the-relational-model
```

Creating, altering, and dropping tables

Now that we know a little about how data is structured in a database, we can learn more about creating our own tables, making changes to them, and even how to delete them.

Using CREATE TABLE

We use the CREATE TABLE command to create tables. For a basic database for an online store, we might have tables for customers, products, orders, product reviews, customer addresses, and more. We can create as many tables as we need, but as mentioned previously, we should give the design some thought so that we don't store duplicate or unused data. That said, don't worry about this too much, as we can always make changes later with the ALTER TABLE command (see the *Using ALTER TABLE* section later in this chapter).

Using CREATE TABLE – basic syntax

The basic syntax of the CREATE TABLE command is as follows:

```
CREATE TABLE table_name (<column_definitions>);
```

As with creating a database, we can add an IF NOT EXISTS command before the table name to suppress the error that would appear if the table exists when we try to create it.

The <column_definitions> part has the following basic syntax:

```
<column_name> <data_type>
    [NOT NULL | NULL]
    [DEFAULT <default_value>]
    [AUTO_INCREMENT]
    [UNIQUE [KEY] | [PRIMARY] KEY]
    [COMMENT '<string>']
```

The parts in angle brackets (`<>`) are the bits that we fill in. The parts in square brackets (`[]`) are optional and the pipe character (`|`) means "or". For example, we can (but do not have to) specify `NULL` or `NOT NULL` in a single column definition but we cannot specify both. Columns are allowed to be `NULL`, or have no value, by default. Marking a column as `NOT NULL` means it can never be undefined; some value has to be assigned to it, even if the value assigned is an empty value. Multiple column definitions are separated by commas.

Using CREATE TABLE – datatypes

There are many different datatypes (given by `<data_type>` in the `column_definitions` syntax example shown previously) to choose from. A datatype is the type of data being stored. Different datatypes exist because various types of data are most efficiently stored in different ways. Plain numbers can be treated differently than dates and vice versa. Common datatypes include numeric (numbers), strings (text), and dates.

Numeric datatypes include `INTEGER` (basic numbers, commonly written as `INT`), and `FLOAT` (for floating point numbers). A good article on floating point numbers can be found at the following location:

```
http://en.wikipedia.org/wiki/Floating_point
```

String (or text-based) datatypes include `CHAR`, `TEXT`, and `VARCHAR`, which are optimized for different lengths of text. The `CHAR` datatype is for fixed-length strings, for example, a product identifier that contains both numbers and letters can't be stored as a number, but if it is a fixed length such as 8 characters, we can store it efficiently as `CHAR(8)`.

The `VARCHAR` datatype is for text that isn't more than a sentence or so long. Text such as names and addresses are commonly stored as `VARCHAR`.

Lastly, date and time datatypes include `DATE`, `TIME`, and `DATETIME`. As you might guess, the `DATE` datatype is for storing dates. Dates are always stored and displayed in the form `YYYY-MM-DD` (a four digit year, a two digit month, and a two digit day), for example `1998-02-14`, and while it is recommended to input them that way, they can be entered in a variety of ways. For example: `2015-5-28`, `15528`, and `15*05*28` are all ways to enter the date `2015-05-28`.

The `TIME` datatype is for time in the format `HH:MM:SS.ssssss` (`hours:minutes:seconds.microseconds`). As with the `DATE` datatype, while MariaDB will store and display values in those formats, it is less picky about how they are entered.

The DATETIME datatype is a combination of both the DATE and TIME datatypes. It stores and displays values in the following form: YYYY-MM-DD HH:MM:SS.ssssss and unlike the TIME datatype, the hours, minutes, and seconds should conform to real-world values (no 26 hour days, for example).

There are other specialized datatypes that can be used with MariaDB, but these are enough to get us started. See a complete list of supported datatypes at the following location:

https://mariadb.com/kb/en/data-types/

> Don't worry about trying to memorize all of the different datatypes now. They'll become second nature as we gain experience using MariaDB.

Using CREATE TABLE– other options

After specifying the type, length, and precision (which are only required for some datatypes), we can specify other options. We can specify whether or not a column is allowed to be undefined (or NULL), what the default value (<default_value> in the syntax example) is, if anything, whether the column auto-increments (only for numeric datatypes such as INT and FLOAT), whether the value in the column should be UNIQUE (meaning whether or not it is allowed to have the same value as the same column in a different row), whether the column is a primary key, and a comment describing the table, if desired.

A primary key is a column, or a group of columns, which uniquely identifies a specific row in the table. No other row in a given table is allowed to have the same primary key. If we try to input a row with a primary key that matches another primary key in the table, we will get an error.

Using CREATE TABLE – an example

For our preceding employees' example, we might use the following CREATE statement to create the table (use the test database or CREATE a new database and then USE it if you want to follow along):

```
CREATE TABLE employees (
    id INT NOT NULL AUTO_INCREMENT PRIMARY KEY,
    surname VARCHAR(100),
    givenname VARCHAR(100),
    pref_name VARCHAR(50),
    birthday DATE COMMENT 'approximate birthday OK'
);
```

When we run the preceding code, the output looks as follows:

```
Query OK, 0 rows affected (0.00 sec)
```

A result of `Query OK` means that the table was created successfully. Zero rows were affected because this is a brand new table and thus has no data in it yet. Unless we are on a very slow, or a very busy server, the command should complete instantly (`0.00` seconds) or near instantly (such as `0.05` seconds).

> Full documentation of the `CREATE TABLE` command can be found at the following location:
> https://mariadb.com/kb/en/create-table/

Using SHOW to display the command used to create a table

At any time, for example, if we want to create a similar table in a different database, we can use the `SHOW CREATE TABLE` command to show a command that will recreate the table exactly. Take a look at the following example:

```
MariaDB [test]> SHOW CREATE TABLE employees \G
*************************** 1. row ***************************
       Table: employees
Create Table: CREATE TABLE `employees` (
  `id` int(11) NOT NULL AUTO_INCREMENT,
  `surname` varchar(100) DEFAULT NULL,
  `givenname` varchar(100) DEFAULT NULL,
  `pref_name` varchar(50) DEFAULT NULL,
  `birthday` date DEFAULT NULL COMMENT 'approximate birthday is OK',
  PRIMARY KEY (`id`)
) ENGINE=InnoDB DEFAULT CHARSET=latin1
1 row in set (0.00 sec)
```

> The \G at the end of the first line in this example is an alternative to using a semicolon (;) and when used it presents the output in a slightly different way, which works well for this example.

The actual CREATE TABLE command that is displayed is slightly different from the CREATE TABLE command that we used to create it, but the table created is exactly the same. The differences exist because MariaDB is giving us enough information to recreate the table exactly, even if we're creating it on a different server with different settings.

For example, the ENGINE and DEFAULT CHARSET parts after the column definitions are default table options on my local MariaDB server. They are specified because on a different MariaDB server, the defaults may be different.

 Full documentation of the SHOW CREATE TABLE command can be found at the following location:
https://mariadb.com/kb/en/show-create-table/

Using DESCRIBE to explore the structure of a table

If we don't necessarily want to look at the commands used to create a table but we want to know the structure of a table, we can use the DESCRIBE command as follows:

```
MariaDB [test]> DESCRIBE employees;
```

Field	Type	Null	Key	Default	Extra
id	int(11)	NO	PRI	NULL	auto_increment
surname	varchar(100)	YES		NULL	
givenname	varchar(100)	YES		NULL	
pref_name	varchar(50)	YES		NULL	
birthday	date	YES		NULL	

```
5 rows in set (0.00 sec)
```

This basic information comes in handy especially when we want to look up information in a table that we are unfamiliar with, or if we can't remember all the fields. (Looking up information is covered in *Chapter 7, Using MariaDB – Selecting, Sorting, and Searching*).

Another thing to note about the DESCRIBE command is that COMMENT is not displayed.

If we are just interested in a specific column, we can specify it as follows:

```
MariaDB [test]> DESCRIBE employees birthday;
+-----------+------+------+-----+---------+-------+
| Field     | Type | Null | Key | Default | Extra |
+-----------+------+------+-----+---------+-------+
| birthday  | date | YES  |     | NULL    |       |
+-----------+------+------+-----+---------+-------+
1 row in set (0.00 sec)
```

 Full documentation of the DESCRIBE command can be found at the following location:
https://mariadb.com/kb/en/describe/

Using ALTER TABLE

We can spend hours, days, and even weeks getting our tables defined just the way we want them, but chances are that at some point, we'll need to make some changes. This is where the ALTER TABLE command comes into play.

Using ALTER TABLE – basic syntax

The basic syntax for the ALTER TABLE command is as follows:

```
ALTER TABLE table_name <alter_definition>[, alter_definition] ...;
```

The <alter_definition> part of the command can ADD, MODIFY, and DROP (delete) columns from tables, among other things. Multiple alter definitions in a single ALTER TABLE command are separated by commas.

Because we can have multiple alter definitions in one ALTER TABLE command, the syntax examples in the next four sections will not contain the beginning ALTER TABLE table_name part that must begin an ALTER TABLE command. The examples that show actual usage will contain the full command.

When using the ALTER TABLE command, the data in our table is preserved and converted when necessary.

Using ALTER TABLE – adding a column

An alter definition of an ALTER TABLE command to add a column has the following pattern:

```
ADD <column_name> <column_definition> [FIRST|AFTER <column_name>]
```

The FIRST and AFTER parts are optional. We can use one, but not both. The FIRST option puts the new column as the first column of a row. The AFTER option lets us specify which column the new column appears after. If we don't use FIRST or AFTER, the column will be added after the current last column. For example, the following will create a new username column and place it after the pref_name column:

```
ALTER TABLE employees ADD username varchar(20) AFTER pref_name;
```

Using ALTER TABLE – modifying a column

An alter definition of an ALTER TABLE command to modify a column has the following pattern:

```
MODIFY <column_name> <column_definition>
```

For example, the following ALTER TABLE command will change the pref_name column to varchar(25) from its original setting of varchar(50):

```
ALTER TABLE employees MODIFY pref_name varchar(25);
```

Using ALTER TABLE – dropping a column

An alter definition of an ALTER TABLE command to drop (delete) a column has the following pattern:

```
DROP <column_name>
```

For example, the following ALTER TABLE command will delete the username column that we created earlier:

```
ALTER TABLE employees DROP username;
```

If you've been following along with these ALTER TABLE commands, your employees table should now look as follows:

```
MariaDB [test]> DESCRIBE employees;

+-----------+--------------+------+-----+---------+----------------+
| Field     | Type         | Null | Key | Default | Extra          |
+-----------+--------------+------+-----+---------+----------------+
| id        | int(11)      | NO   | PRI | NULL    | auto_increment |
| surname   | varchar(100) | YES  |     | NULL    |                |
| givenname | varchar(100) | YES  |     | NULL    |                |
| pref_name | varchar(25)  | YES  |     | NULL    |                |
| birthday  | date         | YES  |     | NULL    |                |
+-----------+--------------+------+-----+---------+----------------+
5 rows in set (0.00 sec)
```

 Full documentation of the ALTER TABLE command is found at the following location:
https://mariadb.com/kb/en/alter-table

Using DROP TABLE

When we no longer need a table, just as when we no longer need a database, we use the DROP TABLE command to delete it. Out of the table commands, this one is by far the easiest, but it is potentially the most dangerous. The basic syntax of the command is as follows:

```
DROP TABLE <table_name>
```

If we try issuing a DROP TABLE on a table that doesn't exist, we will receive an error. We can suppress the error with IF EXISTS. The following are a couple of examples of this:

```
DROP TABLE mytable;
DROP TABLE IF EXISTS mytable;
```

If the table exists, the preceding two commands have the same result, the mytable table is deleted. If the table doesn't exist, the first command will exit with an error and the second command will do nothing.

As mentioned previously, the DROP TABLE command can be very dangerous, because if you have the appropriate permission to drop a table, MariaDB trusts you and will delete the table and everything in it when you tell it to, no questions asked. So when setting up users, it is important to give only a few trusted users, who actually need it, the ability to use the DROP TABLE command. For more on setting up users and giving them permissions, refer *Chapter 4, Administering MariaDB*.

 Full documentation of the DROP TABLE command can be found at the following location:
https://mariadb.com/kb/en/drop-table

Summary

In this chapter, we covered a lot of ground. We learned about the mysql command-line client application and how to use it to connect to MariaDB, how to use the USE command to switch to an existing database, how to use the SHOW command to list all the databases in MariaDB, and how to create our own databases. We also explored a little of the information regarding datatypes and normalization, and learned how to use that information in order to create and modify our own tables. Lastly, we learned how to delete (DROP) both, databases and tables. In the next chapter, we'll start storing and modifying the data in the tables of our database.

6

Using MariaDB – Inserting, Updating, and Deleting

Getting data into the tables in our databases, and updating and deleting that data when necessary, is where we will spend a good portion of our time when working with MariaDB. To learn how to do this, we will be covering the following commands in this chapter:

- Using INSERT
- Using UPDATE
- Using DELETE

Using INSERT

To put data into our database, we use the INSERT command. The basic syntax is as follows:

```
INSERT [INTO] <table_name> [(<column_name>[, <column_name>,...])]
{VALUES | VALUE}
({<expression>|DEFAULT},...)[,(...),...];
```

As with the CREATE TABLE command in the previous chapter, the parts of the syntax example within the angle brackets (<>) are what we'll replace with our own values. The parts between the square brackets ([]) are optional and the pipe character (|) means or. The curly brackets ({}) specify a mandatory section where there is a choice of the key word which you can use. For example, the INTO keyword is optional but makes the INSERT line more readable and we can use the keyword VALUE or VALUES depending on whether we are inserting a single column of information or multiple columns, but we must use one of them. Three dots (. . .) represent the part where the previous part can be repeated.

The `expression` part is the value that we want to put in a column. It could be a calculated value (such as *today's date + four days*), a static value (such as `John`) or it could be the default value assigned to the column (if it has one). Default values are assigned using the key word `DEFAULT`, without any quotes.

Inserting complete rows

As shown in the syntax example, specifying the columns we want to put the data into is optional. For example, to insert a single row into the employees table that we created in the previous chapter, without specifying any column names, we would do the following:

```
INSERT INTO employees VALUES
    (NULL, "Perry", "Lowell Tom", "Tom", "1988-08-05");
```

The downside to not specifying the columns is that we must specify a value for every column in our table, in the order in which they are in the table definition.

For auto-incremented columns, such as the `id` column in our employees table, we have to put something but we can't put in our own value because MariaDB handles that. So, we use `NULL` as a placeholder to let MariaDB know that we are not providing a value and then MariaDB provides its own value. The keyword `NULL`, means no value. Some columns, based on their definition, may not allow us to use `NULL`.

We can use `NULL` for any other column we don't want to insert values into, as long as the column definition allows it. For example, if all we wanted to enter were the surname and given names for a couple of employees, we could do the following:

```
INSERT INTO employees VALUES
    (NULL, "Pratt","Parley", NULL, NULL),
    (NULL, "Snow","Eliza", NULL, NULL);
```

Each row is wrapped in parentheses and multiple rows are separated by commas.

As mentioned previously, the downside to not specifying the columns as a part of an insert statement is that we need to provide something for each column in each row that we are inserting. This can get cumbersome, especially if we have many columns.

More importantly though, in addition to providing something for each column, we also need to list the columns in the exact order that they appear in the database. This presents a safety concern because the order in which the columns appear in our table could change, and if it does, then the values we enter will be put into the wrong columns. For example, our inserts might fail because we're doing something like putting names into our `birthday` column. A worse error would be if the order of the `surname` and the `givenname` columns were switched. Because the data types for those two are the same, no failure will happen if they are in the wrong order in our `INSERT` statement, but will lead to invisible errors and names in the wrong place.

A better and safer method is to always specify the columns that we are inserting data into, even if it is every column in the table.

Inserting partial rows

Often when we are inserting data into a table we only want to insert a few columns, for example, the `surname` and `givenname` columns in our `employees` database. To insert a partial row like this, we specify the columns we want to provide values for, as follows:

```
INSERT INTO employees (surname,givenname) VALUES
    ("Taylor","John"),
    ("Woodruff","Wilford"),
    ("Snow","Lorenzo");
```

Another benefit that we get from specifying specific columns is that we can change the order in which we provide our data (the order in the database will be unchanged). For example, we could list the `pref_name` column as follows:

```
INSERT INTO employees (pref_name,givenname,surname,birthday)
    VALUES ("George","George Albert","Smith","1970-04-04");
```

We can even just specify a single column (in which case we use `VALUE` instead of `VALUES`):

```
INSERT employees (surname) VALUE ("McKay");
```

Full documentation of the `INSERT` command is found at the following location:

https://mariadb.com/kb/en/insert

Inserting from another table

Sometimes, the data we want to insert into a table already exists in another table in our database. To handle this kind of a situation, there is a special form of the INSERT command that we can use. The syntax is as follows:

```
INSERT [INTO] <table_1> [(<column_name>[, <column_name>,...])]
SELECT <column_name>[, <column_name>,...]
FROM <table_2>;
```

For example, suppose we have a table called names in our database, containing employee information from a different company that our company just merged with. Assuming that the data types are compatible with our employees database; the birthdays are stored as dates, the names are compatible with the varchar datatype that our table uses, and so on; we can add the data in that table to our employee table using something similar to the following:

```
INSERT INTO employees (surname, givenname, birthday)
SELECT lastname, firstname, bday
FROM names;
```

When doing an insert like this using the data from another table, we should be careful about trying to insert any auto-incremented columns, such as the id column in the employees database. If the table we are reading from has one of these columns, we either need to verify that there are no values which overlap, or omit it from the data we read as we did in the example.

Don't worry about the SELECT part of the example. The next chapter is all about that command.

 Full documentation of the INSERT...SELECT command is found at the following location:

https://mariadb.com/kb/en/insert-select/

Inserting from a file

Another way to insert data into a table is to read it from a file. One of the most common formats that such files come in is as tab delimited files, where a tab character separates the columns of information. MariaDB has a built-in command that can read these files and insert the data into a table. The basic format is as follows:

```
LOAD DATA [LOCAL] INFILE '<filename>'
    INTO TABLE <tablename>
    [(<column_name>[, <column_name>,...]];
```

If the LOCAL option is used, MariaDB will look for the file on the filesystem that we are running our client on; otherwise it will look in its own filesystem. If we are running the client on the same computer that is running MariaDB, then the LOCAL option does nothing. In either case, it is recommended to give the full path to the file.

If the columns are not specified as part of the command, MariaDB will expect the data in the file to contain every column that the table we are inserting into has, and that they are in the same order. By specifying the columns, we are telling MariaDB what each of the columns in the file are and where they go in our table.

As an example of loading a file, suppose we have a file named new_employees, which has three columns which correspond to the birthday, surname, and givenname columns in our employees table. Look at the following example:

```
1971-08-09    Anderson Neil
1985-01-24    Christofferson Todd
```

To load this file into our employees table, we would do something similar to the following:

```
LOAD DATA INFILE '/tmp/new_employees'
    INTO TABLE employees
    (birthday, surname, givenname);
```

There are many more options for this command, including such things as skipping the first few lines of a file, changing the separator for the columns from tab to something else, and so on.

 Full documentation of the LOAD DATA INFILE command is found at the following location:
https://mariadb.com/kb/en/load-data-infile/

Using UPDATE

Once our data is in a table, we're not done with it. Addresses, names, and many other types of data will change, and when data in a table needs to be updated, we use the UPDATE command. The basic syntax is as follows:

```
UPDATE <table_name>
    SET column_name1={expression|DEFAULT}
    [, column_name2={expression|DEFAULT}] …
    [WHERE <where_conditions>];
```

Unlike the INSERT command, when we are updating data, we specify the data we want to insert right after each column name.

Another difference is the inclusion of a WHERE section. The WHERE section is very important because we use it to specify the exact column or columns of data in the table that we want to change. If we omit the WHERE section, the UPDATE statements will update every instance of that column. For example, we could accidentally change every employee's phone number to the same number when all we wanted to do was to update Gordon's.

 Watch out! Not including the WHERE part in an update statement will tell MariaDB that we want to update every row in our table. We will hardly ever want to do this.

One thing that we should do in our example employees table is to add birthdays and preferred names for some of our employees:

```
UPDATE employees SET
    pref_name = "John", birthday = "1958-11-01"
    WHERE surname = "Taylor" AND givenname = "John";


UPDATE employees SET
    pref_name = "Will", birthday = "1957-03-01"
    WHERE surname="Woodruff";


UPDATE employees SET
    birthday = "1964-04-03"
    WHERE surname = "Snow";
```

For each of the preceding commands, MariaDB should output something similar to the following two lines (the amount of time, 0.03 seconds in the example, may be different):

```
Query OK, 1 row affected (0.03 sec)
Rows matched: 1   Changed: 1   Warnings: 0
```

What these two lines are telling us is that one row matched our WHERE section and that one row was changed.

Also, in these examples, I am looking up employees by `surname`, or by `surname` and `givenname`. If our table contained many thousands of rows in it, representing many thousands of people, there would likely be several people with the same name, so a better `WHERE` section would be something that guaranteed that the person I want to update is the only one that gets updated. This is the purpose and reason behind the ID column in the employees table. This column is set up as the primary key for the table. This means that no other row in the table is allowed to have the same value in that column. It's worth mentioning that a primary key for a table may be defined as multiple columns in a row that, when read together, cannot be the same as any other row in the table.

To find the ID of a specific employee, we would first search for the employee using the `SELECT` command. We'll go over how to do this in the next chapter. Once we have the ID value, we would then use it in our `UPDATE` command. For example, if the Parley Pratt entry had an `id` of 2, we would update his row to add a birthday as follows:

```
UPDATE employees SET
    birthday = "1975-04-12"
    WHERE id = 2;
```

Full documentation of the `UPDATE` command is found at the following location:

https://mariadb.com/kb/en/update/

Using DELETE

Just as data sometimes needs to be updated, sometimes it also needs to be removed from a database table. People get new jobs, products are discontinued, and so on. When the time comes to remove something from a table in our database, we use the `DELETE` command. The basic syntax is as follows:

```
DELETE FROM <table_name> [WHERE <where_conditions>];
```

As with `UPDATE` statements, the `WHERE` part of a `DELETE` statement is optional, but if we leave it off, the command will delete every row in the table, which is even more catastrophic than leaving off the `WHERE` part in an `UPDATE` statement, if such a thing is possible. Make it a habit to always include it.

As an example, let's delete the `Spencer Kimball` employee:

```
DELETE FROM employees
WHERE givenname="Spencer" AND surname="Kimball";
```

As with the UPDATE examples, the WHERE clause is looking up the rows to delete by givenname and surname. A more precise method is to first look up the record to discover its primary key, and then to use that.

Be extremely careful with the DELETE command! It only takes a few seconds to cause hours and even days or weeks of trouble because of a badly written DELETE.

Full documentation of the DELETE command is found at the following location:
https://mariadb.com/kb/en/delete/

Summary

In this chapter, you learned about inserting data into tables as both entire and partial rows, from other tables, and from files, and you also learned about updating and deleting data from our tables.

As mentioned at the beginning of this chapter, inserting, updating, and deleting data is where we will spend a good portion of our time when working with MariaDB. The only thing we will spend more time doing is reading our data, which just so happens to be the focus of the next chapter.

7
Using MariaDB – Retrieving Data

Data is useful only if we can retrieve or read it. In this chapter, we'll learn the basics of reading our data. We will cover the following topics:

- Retrieving data
- Filtering and searching data
- Sorting data
- Joining data
- Summarizing data

Retrieving data

The command for retrieving or reading data from our database is called SELECT. Of all the SQL commands, this is the one which we will probably use most often. The syntax is rather complex, or can be, if we choose to use all the various options. However, the basic syntax is quite simple and is as follows:

```
SELECT <what> FROM <table_name>
    [WHERE <where-conditions>]
    [ORDER BY <column_name>];
```

In the <what> part, we specify the columns that we want to retrieve data from. The WHERE and ORDER BY lines are how we filter and sort our data, respectively.

Complete documentation of the SELECT command, refer to
the following location:
https://mariadb.com/kb/en/select/

Retrieving everything

A common <what> condition is to specify every column. This is done using an
asterisk (*). For example, to retrieve everything from our employees table, we
could do the following:

```
SELECT * FROM employees;
```

Because we have not specified a WHERE clause, everything in the table will be
retrieved; and because we did not specify an ORDER BY clause, the data will be
retrieved and displayed in the order in which it is stored in the table. Depending
on which of the examples in the previous chapter we ran, the output will be similar
to the following:

```
MariaDB [test]> SELECT * FROM employees;

+----+----------------+---------------+-----------+------------+
| id | surname        | givenname     | pref_name | birthday   |
+----+----------------+---------------+-----------+------------+
|  1 | Perry          | Lowell Tom    | Tom       | 1988-08-05 |
|  2 | Pratt          | Parley        | NULL      | 1975-04-12 |
|  3 | Snow           | Eliza         | NULL      | 1964-04-03 |
|  4 | Taylor         | John          | John      | 1958-11-01 |
|  5 | Woodruff       | Wilford       | Will      | 1957-03-01 |
|  6 | Snow           | Lorenzo       | NULL      | 1964-04-03 |
|  7 | Smith          | George Albert | George    | 1970-04-04 |
|  8 | McKay          | NULL          | NULL      | NULL       |
|  9 | Anderson       | Neil          | NULL      | 1971-08-09 |
| 10 | Christofferson | Todd          | NULL      | 1985-01-24 |
+----+----------------+---------------+-----------+------------+
10 rows in set (0.00 sec)
```

Retrieving selected columns

When a table contains lots of columns, or if we are only interested in retrieving some of the data, we might only want to select some of them. This can improve performance a lot, so it's a good idea to use * sparingly and specify individual columns as often as possible. To do so we list the columns, separated by commas, in the <what> section. For example, we could select just the given names and surnames as follows:

```
SELECT givenname,surname FROM employees;
```

The output of this statement will look similar to the following:

```
MariaDB [test]> SELECT givenname,surname FROM employees;
+---------------+----------------+
| givenname     | surname        |
+---------------+----------------+
| Lowell Tom    | Perry          |
| Parley        | Pratt          |
| Eliza         | Snow           |
| John          | Taylor         |
| Wilford       | Woodruff       |
| Lorenzo       | Snow           |
| George Albert | Smith          |
| NULL          | McKay          |
| Neil          | Anderson       |
| Todd          | Christofferson |
+---------------+----------------+
10 rows in set (0.00 sec)
```

Filtering and searching data

In a table with lots of rows, we will probably want to restrict the number of rows that we retrieve. We can do this using one or more WHERE clauses. When filtering, we can use either full and exact column values or partial values.

Filtering by exact values

When filtering by exact values, we use the full value of a column. For example, a WHERE clause to retrieve data about everyone born on or after January 1, 1970 is given as follows:

```
WHERE birthday >= '1970-01-01'
```

The output will look similar to the following:

```
MariaDB [test]> SELECT * FROM employees
    -> WHERE birthday >= '1970-01-01';
+----+----------------+---------------+-----------+------------+
| id | surname        | givenname     | pref_name | birthday   |
+----+----------------+---------------+-----------+------------+
|  1 | Perry          | Lowell Tom    | Tom       | 1988-08-05 |
|  2 | Pratt          | Parley        | NULL      | 1975-04-12 |
|  7 | Smith          | George Albert | George    | 1970-04-04 |
|  9 | Anderson       | Neil          | NULL      | 1971-08-09 |
| 10 | Christofferson | Todd          | NULL      | 1985-01-24 |
+----+----------------+---------------+-----------+------------+
5 rows in set (0.00 sec)
```

The >= sign is a comparison operator. Just like in math, it means greater than or equal to. There are many other comparison operators, and the most common is = (the equals sign) which matches the content of a column exactly. We used these extensively in the previous chapter while updating the data to match specific rows. You can find a complete list of comparison operators at the following location:

https://mariadb.com/kb/en/comparison-operators

The arrow (->) in the previous output example was not something that we typed. The mysql command-line client program inserted it to show that we pressed the *Enter* key before ending our command with a semicolon (;), and so the command that we enter continued on a second line. If we pressed *Enter* and just forgot to end our command, we can just type a semicolon and press *Enter* again. In the previous example, I did it on purpose to split the command into two lines to make it easier to read.

Using logical operators

As mentioned previously, we are not limited to using a single WHERE clause. We can string several of them together, separated by the special AND, OR, IN, and NOT operators.

Using the AND operator

The AND operator adds conditions to our SELECT statement. Both conditions that are separated by an AND operator must match for a row to be fetched. For example:

```
MariaDB [test]> SELECT * FROM employees
    -> WHERE surname = 'Snow'
    -> AND givenname LIKE 'Eli%';
+----+---------+-----------+-----------+------------+
| id | surname | givenname | pref_name | birthday   |
+----+---------+-----------+-----------+------------+
|  3 | Snow    | Eliza     | NULL      | 1964-04-03 |
+----+---------+-----------+-----------+------------+
1 row in set (0.00 sec)
```

There are two people in our employees table with the surname Snow, but with our additional clause and the AND operator, only one is returned.

Using the OR operator

The OR operator is the opposite of the AND operator. If either of the conditions separated by an OR operator match, the row will be fetched. For example:

```
MariaDB [test]> SELECT * FROM employees
    -> WHERE givenname = 'Neil'
    -> OR givenname = 'John';
+----+----------+-----------+-----------+------------+
| id | surname  | givenname | pref_name | birthday   |
+----+----------+-----------+-----------+------------+
|  4 | Taylor   | John      | John      | 1958-11-01 |
|  9 | Anderson | Neil      | NULL      | 1971-08-09 |
+----+----------+-----------+-----------+------------+
2 rows in set (0.00 sec)
```

In the preceding example, if the `givenname` of an employee is either `John` or `Neil`, the row will be fetched.

Evaluation order

In mathematics, there is a concept called 'order of operations', where certain mathematical operations are carried out before others: for example, multiplication before addition. The same concept exists in computer languages, such as SQL.

In SQL, `AND` operators are evaluated first, followed by the `OR` operators. This can cause unexpected behavior if we're not careful. For example:

```
SELECT * FROM employees
  WHERE
        givenname = 'John'
    OR  givenname = 'Tom'
    AND surname = 'Snow';
```

Because of how it is written, we might expect the preceding query to select every row where the `givenname` is either `John` or `Tom` and the surname is `Snow`, and because the two `Snows` in our table are named `Eliza` and `Lorenzo`, we would naturally expect there to be no results returned. But when we run the query, we get the following result:

```
MariaDB [test]> SELECT * FROM employees
  WHERE
    ->       givenname = 'John'
    -> OR    givenname = 'Tom'
    -> AND surname = 'Snow';
+----+---------+-----------+-----------+------------+
| id | surname | givenname | pref_name | birthday   |
+----+---------+-----------+-----------+------------+
|  4 | Taylor  | John      | John      | 1958-11-01 |
+----+---------+-----------+-----------+------------+
1 row in set (0.00 sec)
```

We get a result because of the way MariaDB interprets our query, evaluating `AND` first and then `OR`, means that MariaDB reads our query like this: retrieve a row if the `givenname` equals `Tom` and the surname equals `Snow`, or if the `givenname` equals `John`. There's an employee where the `givenname` is `John`, so that row is matched and retrieved.

A good way to avoid this sort of situation is to group the operations that we want to be together using parentheses, just as we might do in math. If we do that with our example query, grouping the operations on either side of the OR together, we get the following expected result (with no rows returned):

```
MariaDB [test]> SELECT * FROM employees
  WHERE
    ->      (givenname = 'John'
    -> OR   givenname = 'Tom')
    -> AND surname = 'Snow';
Empty set (0.00 sec)
```

Using the IN operator

The IN operator is used to specify a list of values, enclosed in parentheses and separated by commas, that are then compared all at once as if they were separate OR conditions. For example the following two queries are equivalent, but the one using the IN operator is much shorter:

```
SELECT * FROM employees WHERE
    surname = 'Snow'
    OR surname = 'Smith'
    OR surname = 'Pratt';


SELECT * FROM employees WHERE surname IN ('Snow','Smith','Pratt');
```

In both cases, the results retrieved are identical:

```
+----+---------+---------------+-----------+------------+
| id | surname | givenname     | pref_name | birthday   |
+----+---------+---------------+-----------+------------+
|  2 | Pratt   | Parley        | NULL      | 1975-04-12 |
|  3 | Snow    | Eliza         | NULL      | 1964-04-03 |
|  6 | Snow    | Lorenzo       | NULL      | 1964-04-03 |
|  7 | Smith   | George Albert | George    | 1970-04-04 |
+----+---------+---------------+-----------+------------+
```

The IN operator is not just useful for saving space: the values in the list can all be separate SELECT statements, which can help us create powerful and useful queries that change dynamically, based on the current data in our database.

Using the NOT operator

The NOT operator is easy to understand; it simply negates the meaning of the condition that follows it. For example, by adding a NOT operator to our previous IN example, we get a match on every row that does not have a surname of Pratt, Snow, or Smith:

```
MariaDB [test]> SELECT * FROM employees WHERE
    -> surname NOT IN ('Snow','Smith','Pratt');
+----+---------------+-------------+-----------+------------+
| id | surname       | givenname   | pref_name | birthday   |
+----+---------------+-------------+-----------+------------+
|  1 | Perry         | Lowell Tom  | Tom       | 1988-08-05 |
|  4 | Taylor        | John        | John      | 1958-11-01 |
|  5 | Woodruff      | Wilford     | Will      | 1957-03-01 |
|  8 | McKay         | NULL        | NULL      | NULL       |
|  9 | Anderson      | Neil        | NULL      | 1971-08-09 |
| 10 | Christofferson| Todd        | NULL      | 1985-01-24 |
+----+---------------+-------------+-----------+------------+
6 rows in set (0.00 sec)
```

Searching with LIKE

We can also use pattern matching and the LIKE keyword to select rows when we only know some of the information. For example, suppose we want retrieve the record of an employee whose name begins with the letters McK but we don't remember the rest. We can search for this employee using a WHERE clause with the LIKE key word as follows:

```
WHERE surname LIKE "McK%"
```

The output of this example with our employees database is:

```
MariaDB [test]> SELECT * FROM employees
    -> WHERE surname LIKE "McK%";
+----+---------+-----------+-----------+----------+
| id | surname | givenname | pref_name | birthday |
+----+---------+-----------+-----------+----------+
|  8 | McKay   | NULL      | NULL      | NULL     |
+----+---------+-----------+-----------+----------+
1 row in set (0.00 sec)
```

The percent sign (%) in our example is what is known as a wildcard character. It matches zero or more instances of any character or a group of characters. So by specifying the surname pattern McK%, we are saying that we want any surnames that begin with those letters and are followed by zero or more of other characters. This pattern would match values such as McKay, McKinsey, McKool, and even McK.

Simple searching in this way works well for columns without a lot of text in them. If we are storing large amounts of text in our database, full articles or books for example, we will want to look into third-party search tools, such as Sphinx or Elasticsearch.

Sorting data

Our output, by default, is sorted based on the order in which it was inserted into the database. For a list of employees we might want to sort on the surname column. To do this we use an ORDER BY clause. For example:

```
ORDER BY surname
```

Adding this clause to our previous example of everyone born on or after January 1, 1970, our output changes to the following:

```
MariaDB [test]> SELECT * FROM employees
    -> WHERE birthday >= '1970-01-01'
    -> ORDER BY surname;
+----+----------------+---------------+-----------+------------+
| id | surname        | givenname     | pref_name | birthday   |
+----+----------------+---------------+-----------+------------+
|  9 | Anderson       | Neil          | NULL      | 1971-08-09 |
| 10 | Christofferson | Todd          | NULL      | 1985-01-24 |
|  1 | Perry          | Lowell Tom    | Tom       | 1988-08-05 |
|  2 | Pratt          | Parley        | NULL      | 1975-04-12 |
|  7 | Smith          | George Albert | George    | 1970-04-04 |
+----+----------------+---------------+-----------+------------+
5 rows in set (0.00 sec)
```

We can also specify multiple columns, separating each column with a comma. Having a space after the comma, or even before, is optional. For example, the following will order by the surname, then the given name, and finally the birthday:

```
ORDER BY surname,givenname , birthday
```

As our example table is small, the output using this modified WHERE clause is identical to the example where we ordered only by the surname column.

Joining data

The SELECT command is even more powerful when we start using JOIN to gather data from multiple tables. For example, we could do a look up of every employee with their phone numbers for use in a company directory.

For this example, we need to set up an additional table and add some data to it. We'll first create a simple table for the phone numbers, as follows:

```
CREATE TABLE phone (
    id serial PRIMARY KEY,
    emp_id int,
    type char(3),
    cc int(4),
    number bigint,
    ext int);
```

In this table, the emp_id column is where we'll enter a number to match the id column in the employees table. This will relate that row in the phone table to a specific employee.

With the table in place, we then insert some rows, as follows:

```
INSERT INTO phone (emp_id,type,cc,number,ext) VALUES
    (1,'wrk',1,1235551212,23),
    (1,'hom',1,1235559876,NULL),
    (1,'mob',1,1235553434,NULL),
    (2,'wrk',1,1235551212,32),
    (3,'wrk',1,1235551212,11),
    (4,'mob',1,3215559821,NULL),
    (4,'hom',1,3215551234,NULL);
```

With this new table in place, including some example data, we can JOIN data from the employees table to the data in the phone table.

To join data, we specify the columns from both tables, and then list each table in the FROM clause, separated by the type of join we are performing (just JOIN for a simple join), and then an ON clause that defines the two columns we are using to identify which phone records belong to which employees.

For example, the following is what a simple join of the two tables looks like:

```
MariaDB [test]> SELECT surname,givenname,type,cc,number,ext
    -> FROM employees JOIN phone
    -> ON employees.id = phone.emp_id;
+----------+------------+------+------+------------+------+
| surname  | givenname  | type | cc   | number     | ext  |
+----------+------------+------+------+------------+------+
| Perry    | Lowell Tom | wrk  |    1 | 1235551212 |   23 |
| Perry    | Lowell Tom | hom  |    1 | 1235559876 | NULL |
| Perry    | Lowell Tom | mob  |    1 | 1235553434 | NULL |
| Pratt    | Parley     | wrk  |    1 | 1235551212 |   32 |
| Snow     | Eliza      | wrk  |    1 | 1235551212 |   11 |
| Taylor   | John       | mob  |    1 | 3215559821 | NULL |
| Taylor   | John       | hom  |    1 | 3215551234 | NULL |
+----------+------------+------+------+------------+------+
7 rows in set (0.00 sec)
```

In a simple join, any rows in the first table that do not match any rows in the second table are ignored. The first table specified in the FROM clause is called the left table, and the second is called the right table.

To ensure that every employee is listed in our directory, even if they don't have any phone numbers entered in the phone table, we do a LEFT JOIN. For example:

```
SELECT surname,givenname,type,cc,number,ext
    FROM employees LEFT JOIN phone
    ON employees.id = phone.emp_id;
```

The output of the preceding statement will be similar to the following:

```
MariaDB [test]> SELECT surname,givenname,type,cc,number,ext
    -> FROM employees LEFT JOIN phone
    -> ON employees.id = phone.emp_id;
+----------------+----------------+------+------+------------+------+
| surname        | givenname      | type | cc   | number     | ext  |
+----------------+----------------+------+------+------------+------+
| Perry          | Lowell Tom     | wrk  |    1 | 1235551212 |   23 |
| Perry          | Lowell Tom     | hom  |    1 | 1235559876 | NULL |
| Perry          | Lowell Tom     | mob  |    1 | 1235553434 | NULL |
```

Pratt	Parley	wrk	1	1235551212	32
Snow	Eliza	wrk	1	1235551212	11
Taylor	John	mob	1	3215559821	NULL
Taylor	John	hom	1	3215551234	NULL
Woodruff	Wilford	NULL	NULL	NULL	NULL
Snow	Lorenzo	NULL	NULL	NULL	NULL
Smith	George Albert	NULL	NULL	NULL	NULL
McKay	NULL	NULL	NULL	NULL	NULL
Anderson	Neil	NULL	NULL	NULL	NULL
Christofferson	Todd	NULL	NULL	NULL	NULL

```
13 rows in set (0.00 sec)
```

Whenever the `id` column in the `employees` table does not match any rows in the phone table, the columns from the phone table are listed with `NULL` values in the output.

There are other types of joins available, each with their own uses. Full documentation of `JOIN` syntax is found at the following location:

`https://mariadb.com/kb/en/join/`

Summarizing data

Sometimes, we are just looking for information about our data. For this, MariaDB has several built-in functions: `AVG`, `COUNT`, `MIN`, `MAX`, and `SUM`.

The AVG function

The `AVG` function is used for obtaining the average of the data in a column. For example, combined with the `TIMESTAMPDIFF` and `CURDATE` functions, we can use the `AVG` function to calculate the average age of all of the people in the employees table.

The `CURDATE` function doesn't take any arguments and when called, it simply returns the current date.

The `TIMESTAMPDIFF` function takes three arguments — the unit to count by and two dates, and then outputs the difference between the two. The unit is one of several time units, including `MINUTE`, `HOUR`, `DAY`, `WEEK`, `MONTH`, `QUARTER`, and `YEAR`.

The `TIMESTAMPDIFF` and `CURDATE` functions are just two of several functions that make working with dates and times easier. Find out more about them at the following location:

```
https://mariadb.com/kb/en/date-and-time-functions/
```

Putting all three functions together we get the following:

```
SELECT AVG(TIMESTAMPDIFF(YEAR,birthday,CURDATE()))
FROM employees;
```

Depending on when you run this statement and the dates in the birthday column, the average you get back will be different.

The COUNT function

The COUNT function is often used to count the number of rows returned by a query. For example, to count the number of rows in the `employees` table, we would type the following command:

```
SELECT COUNT(*) FROM employees;
```

Doing this is a little silly on a table like ours, which only has a few rows; after all, the output of `SELECT * FROM employees;` includes a line at the very end telling us the number of rows returned, and thus the number of rows in the table. But, for a table with tens of thousands or even millions of rows, this function is a much better way of finding out the number of rows.

Another use of COUNT is to discover how many rows have a value in a specific column. For example, not every row in our table has a preferred name set; to count how many do have a set preferred name, we can run the following command:

```
SELECT COUNT(pref_name) FROM employees;
```

The MIN and MAX functions

These two functions determine the minimum and maximum values. For example, the oldest employee can be determined with a double SELECT statement, where we look up an employee using the output of the function as follows:

```
SELECT * FROM employees
   WHERE birthday = (SELECT MIN(birthday) from employees);
```

The output of the preceding command will look similar to the following:

```
MariaDB [test]> SELECT * FROM employees
    -> WHERE birthday = (SELECT MIN(birthday) FROM employees);
+----+----------+-----------+-----------+------------+
| id | surname  | givenname | pref_name | birthday   |
+----+----------+-----------+-----------+------------+
|  5 | Woodruff | Wilford   | Will      | 1957-03-01 |
+----+----------+-----------+-----------+------------+
1 row in set (0.00 sec)
```

And likewise, the youngest employee can be determined by using MAX instead of MIN in the example as follows:

```
MariaDB [test]> SELECT * FROM employees
    -> WHERE birthday = (SELECT MAX(birthday) FROM employees);
+----+----------+-----------+-----------+------------+
| id | surname  | givenname | pref_name | birthday   |
+----+----------+-----------+-----------+------------+
|  1 | Perry    | Lowell Tom | Tom      | 1988-08-05 |
+----+----------+-----------+-----------+------------+
1 row in set (0.00 sec)
```

> In the two previous examples where there are two SELECT queries, one inside the other, the inside query is called a subquery. We will not be covering them in this book, but if you'd like to learn more about them, check out the *Subqueries* section of the MariaDB Knowledge Base by going to:
> https://mariadb.com/kb/en/subqueries/

The SUM function

The SUM function is used to compute the total of a set of values. For example, we could total up the combined ages of every employee with something like the following using the TIMESTAMPDIFF and CURDATE functions. This is similar to what we did with the AVG function to convert a birth date into an employee's age.

```
SELECT SUM(TIMESTAMPDIFF(YEAR,birthday,CURDATE()))
FROM employees;
```

Computing combined ages is not very useful. But for other tables, such as an orders table, the SUM function would come in very handy for finding out, for example, how many widgets a specific customer has ordered in the last year.

Using GROUP BY with summarized data

Sometimes, the rows in our database contain natural groups of data. For example, the number of red or blue shirts ordered. The GROUP BY clause can be used with summary functions to group like data together.

In our employees database, we can use GROUP BY with the COUNT function to find out which surnames are the most popular as follows:

```
SELECT surname, COUNT(*)
    FROM employees
    GROUP BY surname;
```

The output of the preceding command will look similar to the following:

```
MariaDB [test]> SELECT surname, COUNT(*)
    -> FROM employees
    -> GROUP BY surname;
+----------------+----------+
| surname        | COUNT(*) |
+----------------+----------+
| Anderson       |        1 |
| Christofferson |        1 |
| McKay          |        1 |
| Perry          |        1 |
| Pratt          |        1 |
| Smith          |        1 |
| Snow           |        2 |
| Taylor         |        1 |
| Woodruff       |        1 |
+----------------+----------+
9 rows in set (0.00 sec)
```

Using HAVING to filter GROUP BY

The previous GROUP BY example outputs all the surnames with a count of how many times each surname is used. Most of them are only used once, so since we are trying to determine which surnames are used the most, it makes sense to filter out the ones that are only used once. To do this, we add a HAVING clause after the GROUP BY clause as follows:

```
SELECT surname, COUNT(*)
    FROM employees
    GROUP BY surname
    HAVING COUNT(*) > 1;
```

The HAVING clause eliminates most of the results, leading to a more readable output:

```
MariaDB [test]> SELECT surname, COUNT(*)
    -> FROM employees
    -> GROUP BY surname
    -> HAVING COUNT(*) > 1;
+---------+----------+
| surname | COUNT(*) |
+---------+----------+
| Snow    |        2 |
+---------+----------+
1 row in set (0.00 sec)
```

In a larger table, we may want to filter out the names used only two to three times, to keep the number of rows returned manageable.

The HAVING clause is a filter similar to WHERE, and so it can use any of the various comparison operators.

Summary

In this chapter, you learned how to retrieve data, either all the data in a table or just some of it. You also learned how to filter the data so that you only get the parts you're looking for, by sorting, summarizing, grouping, and manipulating your retrieved data, and by using operators to retrieve rows more selectively.

With this, and the previous two chapters, we are now familiar with the basic SQL database **Create, Read, Update, and Delete (CRUD)** operations that will be part of nearly all of our interactions in MariaDB.

In *Chapter 8, Maintaining MariaDB*, you will learn how to keep your database running smoothly.

8
Maintaining MariaDB

Similar to houses and cars, databases need to be maintained if they are to run smoothly. In this chapter, we'll cover the following maintenance-related topics:

- MariaDB log files
- Optimizing and tuning MariaDB
- Backing up, importing, and restoring data
- Repairing MariaDB

MariaDB log files

Depending on how we configure it, MariaDB will keep very detailed or very sparse logs. The location of these logs is configured in our `my.cnf` (`my.ini` on Windows) MariaDB configuration file. On Linux, the default location is `/var/log/mysql/` and on Windows, the default location is in the MariaDB data directory.

There are several different kinds of logs, each kind serving a different purpose.

The binary log

The MariaDB binary log is a series of files that contain events. An event is a description of any modification to the contents of our database. As indicated by the name, and unlike most other kinds of log files, MariaDB binary log files are in a binary format. They are not readable by us unless we use a helper program such as `mysqlbinlog`.

The binary log is controlled by the `log_bin` variable. The main purpose of the variable is to turn binary logging on and off. Basically, if the variable is present in the `[mysqld]` or `[server]` sections of our configuration file, binary logging will be turned on, and if it isn't, binary logging will be turned off. An optional function of this variable is to set the name and location of the binary log. The following is an example:

```
log_bin = /var/log/mysql/mariadb-bin
```

MariaDB will take the name and add numbers to the end of the actual files which it writes to. The following is an example of using the `mysqlbinlog` program to display the contents of a binary log in human readable text:

```
mysqlbinlog /var/log/mysql/mariadb-bin.000269
```

Each event in a binary log file is preceded with some comment lines that give the date and time of the event, and its position in the log.

Apart from its informational value, the MariaDB binary log has some other uses. First, it can be used for recovery after a server crash. It is also used when replicating from one server to another. When used for replication, they are transferred to the slave servers as relay logs, but they are basically the same as regular binary logs and can be read with the `mysqlbinlog` program.

> More information about the binary log can be found at the following location:
> https://mariadb.com/kb/en/binary-log/

The error log

The error log is where MariaDB logs information about critical errors. This is also where MariaDB records startup and shutdown information. If MariaDB crashes or fails to start, this is the log where we should look first.

We can control the location using the `log_error` variable, which, like other logging variables, is placed in the `[mysqld]` or `[server]` sections of our configuration files. The following is an example of this:

```
log_error = /var/log/mysql/error.log
```

The default configuration files shipped with MariaDB on Linux configure this file to be at this location, but it can be placed elsewhere.

Unlike the binary log, the absence of this variable does not turn error logging off. If the location is not configured in our `my.cnf` or `my.ini` file, error logging is still enabled and the default location is the data directory. Also, the default name will be `hostname.err`, where the hostname is the name of the computer that MariaDB is running on.

More information about the error log can be found at the following location:

`https://mariadb.com/kb/en/error-log/`

The general query log

The general query log is disabled by default. This is because the general query log, when enabled, stores a record of every query that MariaDB receives, including queries that don't change any data. This is in contrast to the binary log, which only stores queries that change data. On a busy server with lots of users, storing all queries can lead to lots of huge log files very quickly, so it is usually not necessary nor recommended to enable this log.

However, if we are trying to discover a hidden performance bottleneck or absolutely need a record of everything that the server is doing, this log can be enabled with the `general_log` and `general_log_file` variables. The first is used to explicitly turn the general log on (`=1`) or off (`=0`). The second configures where we want the log to be and what we want it to be called. The following example turns the general query log on and stores it at `/var/log/mysql/mysql.log`:

```
general_log = 1
general_log_file = /var/log/mysql/mysql.log
```

If we are only interested in queries that change data, the only log we need to look at is the binary log and we do not need to enable the general query log. As it says in a comment in the default `my.cnf` file shipped with MariaDB, the general log is a performance killer, so we should only enable it if we need to, and only for short periods of time.

More information about the general query log can be found at the following location:

`https://mariadb.com/kb/en/general-query-log/`

The slow query log

The MariaDB slow query log, when enabled, contains a record of queries that take longer than a configured amount of time to run. This log is very useful when tuning and optimizing MariaDB as it stores a lot of useful information, such as the time it took to execute a long query, the user who executed the query, the hostname the user came from, and other details.

This log is disabled by default. To enable it, we add the following to the [mysqld] or [server] sections of our my.cnf or my.ini config file:

```
slow_query_log = 1
```

There are four other variables that we use to control the behavior of the slow query log. We use the slow_query_log_file variable to set the location of the log file.

The long_query_time variable sets the amount of time a query has to run before MariaDB considers it to be slow. Time can be expressed in whole seconds down to microsecond precision (0.000001).

The log_slow_rate_limit variable is used to control how often long queries are actually logged. For example, a setting of 20 would log every twentieth slow query, or 5 percent of the slow queries. This is useful if our slow query log is growing too fast. If this variable is not present, the default is for the slow query log to log every slow query.

Lastly, the log_slow_verbosity variable controls what information is logged, with multiple values separated by commas (,). Possible values for this variable are as follows:

- microtime: This logs queries in microseconds
- query_plan: This logs query execution plan information
- innodb: This adds additional statistical information about queries that touch the XtraDB and InnoDB tables
- standard: This turns on both the microtime and innodb variables
- full: This turns on all values
- profiling: This allows the logged queries to be profiled

The following example turns on the slow query log and sets some common options:

```
slow_query_log = 1
slow_query_log_file = /var/log/mysql/mariadb-slow.log
long_query_time = 0.05
log_slow_rate_limit = 30
log_slow_verbosity = query_plan,standard
```

More information about the slow query log can be found at the following location:

```
https://mariadb.com/kb/en/slow-query-log/
```

Optimizing and tuning MariaDB

Tuning and optimizing MariaDB, and the applications that connect to it, for maximum performance is a subject worthy of a book in itself. We won't go into the details of specific strategies here because it's generally not necessary when we're just getting started with MariaDB. But it is useful to know a little about the subject, which is the purpose of this section.

The basic process of tuning and optimizing MariaDB starts with identifying the choke points: that is, the places that are causing unnecessary slowdowns. Using the `slow query log` discussed previously in this chapter, to identify these choke points is a good place to start.

Once a problem query, or set of queries, has been identified, the next step is to implement a fix of some sort. This could be as simple as rewriting the query to be more efficient, or the query could be sped up by adding an index to the table.

We can also gather and examine user and table statistics to identify patterns of usage that we can potentially optimize. Or we can examine our table definitions to see if there are any tweaks that can be made there to make things faster or more efficient. The list of ways to squeeze more performance out of MariaDB is nearly endless.

If the query and our database are as optimized as we can make them, there are still things that we can do. Hardware, for example, can be a limitation. A busy database that needs to respond quickly needs to be on fast hardware. Fast disks, lots of memory, and a fast processor are all important ways we can improve MariaDB's performance without changing anything in the database itself.

More information on optimizing and tuning MariaDB can be found at the following location:

```
https://mariadb.com/kb/en/optimization-and-tuning/
```

Backing up, importing, and restoring data

MariaDB ships with a couple of utilities that can be used to back up our databases. Data in MariaDB is written to special files on disk, so it may be tempting to think that we can just make a copy of the MariaDB data directory and be done with it. The problem with this is that the data files are always open and in use while MariaDB is running and problems can arise if we try to back up the files directly. At the end of this section, we will describe a method for taking backups of the data directory, but first, we'll go over conventional backup techniques.

Basic backups with mysqldump

By default, the `mysqldump` client backup utility generates SQL backups. These backups are in a text format and contain all the necessary SQL commands to recreate tables and restore the data in those tables.

There are many options, but the basic syntax is as follows:

```
mysqldump [-u username] [-p] database_name [table_name]
```

If `table_name` is not given, `mysqldump` will back up all the tables in the named database. For example, the following command will back up the entire test database:

```
mysqldump -u root -p test > test.sql
```

The output of `mysqldump` goes to standard out. When running the command from a terminal, it will be echoed directly to the screen. So in the preceding example command, we use the > redirect character to direct the output into a file named `test.sql` (overwriting the file if it already exists).

Restoring backups made with mysqldump

To restore the preceding backup, we can use the `mysql` command-line client as follows:

```
mysql -u root -p test < test.sql
```

As with the `mysqldump` example, we use a redirect character, but this time it is redirecting in the opposite direction (<), that is, from the `test.sql` file to the `mysql` client. The `mysql` client reads the file and executes all of the SQL commands in turn, restoring the backed up tables and their data.

Making tab-delimited backups with mysqldump

We can also use `mysqldump` to create tab-delimited files. This is done using the `--tab` option. When using this option, `mysqldump` will create two files. A `tablename.sql` file with the SQL commands to recreate the table, and a `tablename.txt` file with the actual data in tab-delimited format. The following is an example of using `mysqldump` and `--tab` to backup up the employees table in our test database:

```
mysqldump --tab /tmp/ -u root -p test employees
```

The `--tab` option needs a directory after it where it can write the files. The SQL file is owned by whichever user we used to run the `mysqldump` command. The TXT file, on the other hand, is owned by the `mysql` user, so whatever directory we specify needs to have permissions so that both users can write to it. The `/tmp/` directory in Linux is used in the example because, by default, this directory can be written to by anyone.

So why would a tab-delimited file of our data be useful? Well, for starters, the `mysqlimport` program reads tab-delimited files. Popular spreadsheets also read and write to tab-delimited files. So, for example, if we've been keeping our data in a spreadsheet, and have decided to move it to a MariaDB database, we can export our spreadsheet data as a tab-delimited file, create the tables in MariaDB, and then use `mysqlimport` to import our data. At a later point, we could use `mysqldump` to dump the data or a subset of the data to a file and then open it with our spreadsheet program, and create some nice pie charts or other graphs.

There are scores of other options that we can use to tweak and customize what and how `mysqldump` backs up our data. It's well worth your time to learn all of these many options.

[Full documentation of the `mysqldump` utility is found at the following location:

https://mariadb.com/kb/en/mysqldump/]

Restoring and importing data with mysqlimport

We talked briefly about `mysqlimport` in the previous section. In short, this command is used to import data into MariaDB. This data could be a backup that we made previously or completely new data. There are several options for this, but the basic syntax is as follows:

```
mysqlimport [--local] [-u username] [-p] database_name filename
```

The `filename` attribute must be the name of the table we want to import into. The `--local` option tells `mysqlimport` to read from the local filesystem instead of from the data directory of the server.

The following example imports the `employees.txt` file that we generated earlier:

```
mysqlimport --local -u root -p test /tmp/employees.txt
```

Any records that cannot be imported will be skipped, and `mysqlimport` will report this and generate a warning. An example would be a situation where our file has a column in it that contains values that must be unique in our table, but some of them match existing records in the table.

> Full documentation of the `mysqlimport` utility is found at the following location:
>
> https://mariadb.com/kb/en/mysqlimport

Making backups of MyISAM tables with mysqlhotcopy

The `mysqlhotcopy` backup program is actually a Perl script. It can take backups quickly, but only if our tables use the `MyISAM` or `ARCHIVE` storage engines.

An easy way to show the storage engines being used by the tables in our database is with the following `SELECT` statement:

```
SELECT TABLE_NAME,ENGINE
    FROM information_schema.tables
    WHERE TABLE_SCHEMA="test";
```

We can change `test` to the name of whichever database we want to check.

The default storage engine for MariaDB is InnoDB, so this script is less useful than it used to be several years ago when MyISAM was the default storage engine. If we do have MyISAM tables, however, it remains a useful tool.

The basic syntax of the mysqlhotcopy command is as follows:

```
mysqlhotcopy db_name [/path/to/new_directory]
```

If the path to a new directory is not given, mysqlhotcopy will write the backup to the MariaDB data directory. Writing a backup to the data directory is not recommended, so be sure to always specify a path.

Other limitations are that the command must be run by a user who can read the data files in the data directory, and if we use a password when connecting to MariaDB, we must specify it on the command line or in a my.cnf file as mysqlhotcopy does not prompt us for the password.

> Full documentation of the mysqlhotcopy program is found at the following location:
> https://mariadb.com/kb/en/mysqlhotcopy/

Making backups of XtraDB and InnoDB tables with xtrabackup

The xtrabackup backup program is made specifically for use with XtraDB and InnoDB tables. It can take quick, full backups of our databases while MariaDB is running.

Creating a backup with xtrabackup is a multi-step process. First we take a backup and then we prepare the backup so that it is ready to be restored when necessary. To take a backup, we do the following:

```
xtrabackup --backup \
  --datadir=/var/lib/mysql/ --target-dir=/path/to/backup/
```

The --datadir option should point at the location of our MariaDB data files; on Linux the default data directory location is /var/lib/mysql/. On Linux, we will also need to preface the command with sudo.

InnoDB and XtraDB tables are stored across several files, and backups made with xtrabackup are the same. This is why while taking a backup with xtrabackup, we specify a directory and not a file name with the --target-dir option.

While a backup is being made, xtrabackup will print various bits of information to let us know how the backup is progressing. Backups may take a long time if we have a lot of data and/or if our server is very busy.

After making a raw backup, we need to prepare the backup so that it can be restored if necessary. The reason we need to do this is because of the way that xtrabackup and InnoDB and XtraDB tables work. If we try to restore using a raw backup that hasn't been prepared, it is very likely that MariaDB will refuse to start.

To prepare the backup we just made so that it is ready for restoring, we run the following command twice:

```
xtrabackup --prepare --target-dir=/path/to/backup/
```

The first time that we run xtrabackup with the --prepare option, our backed up data will be cleaned up and put into a logical order. The second time that the --prepare option is used, xtrabackup will create some log files that help speed up restoring our data, if it turns out that we need to do that. Running --prepare a third, fourth, or any more number of times won't do anything, but is safe to do so in case we can't remember if we've run it for the second time.

> Full documentation of xtrabackup, including installation instructions, is available at the following location:
> http://www.percona.com/doc/percona-xtrabackup/

Restoring backups made with xtrabackup

The easiest way to restore from a backup made with xtrabackup is to use a utility, such as rsync or the cp command, to copy all the files in the backup directory to our MariaDB data directory. Before doing so, we must stop MariaDB and then run the rsync or cp command. Here's an example rsync command:

```
rsync -avP /path/to/backup/ /var/lib/mysql/
```

After the files are copied back to the MariaDB data directory, and before we start MariaDB, it's a good idea to make sure that the ownership of the files is correct. By default in most Linux distributions, the default user and group are called mysql, so this can be done with something similar to the following:

```
chown -R mysql:mysql /var/lib/mysql/
```

Making cold backups

Another option for backing up MariaDB is to just copy the entire data directory. This is called a cold backup. As mentioned at the beginning of this section, problems can arise if we try to do this while MariaDB is running. But if we stop MariaDB briefly, and are using a filesystem that supports snapshots (called shadow volume copies on Windows), we can stop MariaDB briefly, make a snapshot, and then restart MariaDB. Total downtime for an operation such as this, depending on various factors, might be only a few seconds. The snapshotted directory may then be backed up in a simialr way to any other filesystem directory backup.

This is obviously not an ideal way to take backups in all situations, especially when stopping the database server, even for a few seconds, is not an option. But it can work very well in some cases.

Repairing MariaDB

After a hardware failure, a power outage, or even after an upgrade, it is a good idea to check the tables in our MariaDB databases to make sure they are all right. MariaDB includes several utilities for doing this.

Checking and optimizing tables with mysqlcheck

The `mysqlcheck` program can check, analyze, optimize, and repair the MariaDB database tables. Basic syntax for the command is as follows:

```
mysqlcheck [options] [-u username] [-p] database_name [table_name]
```

Here is an example of running the command to check our test database, and its output:

```
daniel@gandalf:~$ mysqlcheck -u root -p test
Enter password:
test.employees                                          OK
```

We can specify multiple databases using the `--databases` option as follows:

```
mysqlcheck -u root -p --databases db_name1 db_name2 db_name3
```

We can also tell the program to check all our databases with the `--all-databases` option, as follows:

```
mysqlcheck -u root -p --all-databases
```

By default, `mysqlcheck` will only perform basic checks when it is run. To get it to optimize, analyze, or repair tables, we use one of the following options:

```
--optimize
--analyze
--repair
```

Not all of the options work on all tables. For example, `InnoDB` tables cannot be repaired with `mysqlcheck`. The program displays an error message if it cannot perform a requested action.

> Full documentation of the `mysqlcheck` utility is found at the following location:
>
> https://mariadb.com/kb/en/mysqlcheck/

Repairing tables

Thankfully, MariaDB is a very mature and stable program, and problems are few and very far between. However, power does sometimes go out and hardware sometimes fails catastrophically or gradually, so there may come a time when a table in our database has problems and needs to be repaired.

`MyISAM` and `Aria` tables can often be repaired with the `mysqlcheck` program, so if `mysqlcheck` reports that a table needs repairing then we can usually simply re-run the program with the `--repair` option as described previously in this section. Unfortunately, `mysqlcheck` cannot repair `InnoDB` tables.

However, `InnoDB` and `XtraDB` are crash safe, which means that they are protected to a certain extent when failures do occur. This protection means that the chances of a hardware failure causing corruption are very low. `InnoDB` and `XtraDB` also have a built-in crash recovery mechanism. The way to use it is to add the `innodb_force_recovery` option to the `[mysqld]` section of our `my.cnf` or `my.ini` file set to a number between `1` and `6`. Setting this variable to `0`, or removing it entirely, disables it. While this option is set, MariaDB will not allow any `InnoDB` tables to be changed. The higher the number, the more aggressively MariaDB will try to repair the tables. Full documentation of this feature is available at the following location:

https://mariadb.com/kb/en/xtradbinnodb-recovery-modes/

If `innodb_force_recovery` does not work, we may need to dump and reload our affected tables. This procedure can take a long time on a large server, so it should only be used as a last resort. The basic procedure to dump and reload a database is the same as we went over in the `mysqldump` section previously, but here it is again:

```
mysqldump [options] database_name > dump.sql
mysql database_name < dump.sql
```

So to dump and reload our test database, we might do the following:

```
mysqldump -u root -p test > dump.sql
mysql -u root -p test < dump.sql
```

This reload process is more likely to succeed if it is used in conjunction with the `innodb_force_recovery` variable. For example, a setting of 1 tells `InnoDB` and `XtraDB` to skip the corrupt indexes and records instead of attempting to read them. Refer to the `XtraDB`/`InnoDB` recovery modes page in the MariaDB Knowledge Base found previously in this section for more information.

If the preceding reload process doesn't fix the error, we might want to call in some experts. There are various other recovery strategies out there, but they are beyond the scope of this book. We could also try reloading from a backup; we may lose some data depending on how old the backup is, but losing some data is better than losing everything.

Summary

In this chapter, you learned about the various MariaDB log files, what they are, and how to use them. We looked at how to take different kinds of backups and how to restore our data from those backups, and we briefly discussed optimization. Lastly, we wrapped up this chapter with a discussion of the various things we can do if something goes wrong and we need to repair or dump and reload the tables in our database.

MariaDB Next Steps

This book provides an introduction to MariaDB with enough information to get us started. MariaDB is a large system with many parts, options, and capabilities.

So where do we go from here? If we have a question, where do we go for help?

Here is a list of the various online resources available to help us on our way to becoming a MariaDB expert.

Let's begin with the official MariaDB website. MariaDB downloads, the MariaDB Foundation blog, and other official MariaDB information can be found at the following location:

```
http://mariadb.org
```

Next is the MariaDB Knowledge Base found at the following location:

```
https://mariadb.com/kb
```

The MariaDB Knowledge Base is the official location of the MariaDB documentation. New information is added here on a daily basis. Whenever something is added to or changed in MariaDB, it is documented here. Release notes and change logs for MariaDB releases are also posted here.

There is also an *Ask a Question* feature that can be used if we have a question about something in MariaDB. We just navigate to the section or the item that we are interested in, click on the button and ask away. We can also provide our own tips and tricks by leaving comments on the page. Registration is required (to cut down on spam), but it is free and all content is released under a Creative Commons, GFDL, or GPL license.

If we need to talk to someone immediately there are, again, a few options. First is IRC, where we can engage in real-time chat conversations with other users and with the developers of MariaDB. The official MariaDB channel is #maria on the Freenode IRC network. See the knowledge base entry on IRC (https://mariadb.com/kb/en/irc) for more information.

There are also three official MariaDB e-mail lists: a developers list for technical discussions about MariaDB development, a discuss list for general discussions about using MariaDB, and a docs list for discussion and planning related to the MariaDB documentation. All three lists are hosted on launchpad.net. The most useful list for end users is the discuss list. Following are the links to these lists:

- MariaDB developers list (https://launchpad.net/~maria-developers)
- MariaDB discuss list (https://launchpad.net/~maria-discuss)
- MariaDB docs list (https://launchpad.net/~maria-docs)

Lastly, MariaDB is active on the major social media platforms. Following are the locations of the official MariaDB accounts on Twitter, Google+, and Facebook:

- Twitter (http://twitter.com/mariadb)
- Google+ (http://google.com/+mariadb)
- Facebook (http://fb.com/MariaDB.dbms)

I hope you enjoy working with MariaDB!

Index

Thank you for buying
Getting Started with MariaDB
Second Edition

About Packt Publishing

Packt, pronounced 'packed', published its first book, *Mastering phpMyAdmin for Effective MySQL Management*, in April 2004, and subsequently continued to specialize in publishing highly focused books on specific technologies and solutions.

Our books and publications share the experiences of your fellow IT professionals in adapting and customizing today's systems, applications, and frameworks. Our solution-based books give you the knowledge and power to customize the software and technologies you're using to get the job done. Packt books are more specific and less general than the IT books you have seen in the past. Our unique business model allows us to bring you more focused information, giving you more of what you need to know, and less of what you don't.

Packt is a modern yet unique publishing company that focuses on producing quality, cutting-edge books for communities of developers, administrators, and newbies alike. For more information, please visit our website at www.packtpub.com.

About Packt Open Source

In 2010, Packt launched two new brands, Packt Open Source and Packt Enterprise, in order to continue its focus on specialization. This book is part of the Packt Open Source brand, home to books published on software built around open source licenses, and offering information to anybody from advanced developers to budding web designers. The Open Source brand also runs Packt's Open Source Royalty Scheme, by which Packt gives a royalty to each open source project about whose software a book is sold.

Writing for Packt

We welcome all inquiries from people who are interested in authoring. Book proposals should be sent to author@packtpub.com. If your book idea is still at an early stage and you would like to discuss it first before writing a formal book proposal, then please contact us; one of our commissioning editors will get in touch with you.

We're not just looking for published authors; if you have strong technical skills but no writing experience, our experienced editors can help you develop a writing career, or simply get some additional reward for your expertise.

open source
community experience distilled

Mastering MariaDB

ISBN: 978-1-78398-154-0   Paperback: 384 pages

Debug, secure, and back up your data for optimum server performance with MariaDB

1. Monitor database activity and the major operating system parameters to improve performance.

2. Tweak the behavior of a large number of servers to achieve the desired level of stability and reliability.

3. Solve the typical problems related to running a server, such as slow queries, long locks, and so on.

MariaDB Cookbook

ISBN: 978-1-78328-439-9   Paperback: 282 pages

Over 95 recipes to unlock the power of MariaDB

1. Enable performance-enhancing optimizations.

2. Connect to different databases and file formats.

3. Filled with clear step-by-step instructions that can be run on a live database.

Please check **www.PacktPub.com** for information on our titles

Getting Started with MariaDB

ISBN: 978-1-78216-809-6   Paperback: 100 pages

Learn how to use MariaDB to store your data easily and hassle-free

1. A step-by-step guide to installing and configuring MariaDB.

2. Includes real-world examples that help you learn how to store and maintain data on MariaDB.

3. Written by someone who has been involved with the project since its inception.

MariaDB High Performance

ISBN: 978-1-78398-160-1   Paperback: 298 pages

Familiarize yourself with the MariaDB system and build high-performance applications

1. Build multiple slaves and load balance with HA-Proxy.

2. Explore MariaDB 10 features like GTID replication or Sharding using Spider.

3. This is a step-by-step tutorial guide to help you build high-performance applications.

Made in the USA
San Bernardino, CA
23 March 2016